THE JOURNEY

A FAMILY'S STORY OF LOVE, LOSS, AND RESTORATION

ALEX GABBI

The Journey

First edition published in November, 2014

First printing in November, 2014

www.alexgabbi.com

ISBN-13: 978-1502889263

ISBN-10: 1502889269

To Heather, for loving me, believing in me, and making me into the man I am today.

To Nico, Maya and Luca, for being the brightest light at the end of my tunnel. I will always love you more than you could ever imagine.

CONTENTS

FOREWARD

I never really thought I would write again. I had been a prolific writer in my teens and early twenties. Then one day it had just stopped. My ability vanished almost overnight. From that moment on, I hadn't been able to produce a single significant page of prose in 20 years.

Then I met Chris Martin. At the time, he worked with a company named Myriad. He had been commissioned to make a video of me telling the story of my wife, Heather Gabbi. It would be called "Fireworks" in honor of Independence Day, the day that she died of cancer.

Chris had been an Executive Producer for several renowned TV shows and was 'stereotypical' East Coast. We hit it off immediately.

After our day of filming, the next morning Chris told me that he had never met anyone who had dealt with the loss of a loved one in such a thoughtful, noble, and wonderful way. He suggested I tell my story more fully.

A few months later, it hit me that Chris was absolutely right. Whether anyone else ever even read it, the idea of writing my story somehow felt liberating, therapeutic and healing. So I started writing. And for the first time in over 20 years, it came easily. The book just flowed. Every day I would find I had something new to say, add or embellish. I kept writing until I realized one day that I had nothing left to say.

This is a book that is just as much about a man personally healing from a tragic loss as it is about a work that I hope will inspire others to heal and overcome. If after reading this book, you find yourself wanting to extract just a little more out of a day, or laugh a little louder, or love a little more freely, then I will have been successful in my endeavor.

I would like to thank Heather most of all. She was the love of my life and formed me in great part into the man I am today. She taught me to always look for the silver lining, be inquisitive and live life with passion. She also made me realize that what you do for others defines you so much more than anything you could ever do for yourself.

I would like to thank my three wonderful children – Nico, Maya and Luca. They have made every single day since their mother's passing worth living – even the darkest ones. Seeing the wonderful people they continue to grow into makes me proud to be their father and realize that their mother is alive and well within their hearts and minds.

I would like to acknowledge my parents for helping lighten the burdens I carried in my greatest times of need and for being wonderful grandparents to the kids. I am equally grateful to Heather's family for ensuring that the huge void left by her was filled and that we all remained united.

Finally, I want to thank all of our friends. They fought valiantly with us and were here to help ensure the pieces got picked up after Heather's death. I will be forever indebted to them for the role they played in helping Heather live and just as importantly for having the courage to help her die. I love you all for it and will never forget it.

I would like to extend a special heart-felt thank you to the following individuals and organizations:

Myriad, for very early on affording me with the opportunity to recognize there could be a light at the end of the tunnel;

Wonders & Worries, for helping my children through the darkest moment of their lives;

Scott, my brother from another mother. I will always hate you the least;

Jim, for reminding me that vis-à-vis was always my lucky phrase vis-à-vis all other phrases;

Ximena, for being there when Maya needed you and for always loving on your Queenie;

Cynthia, for always knowing when it was the right time to give a hug, and for being there literally every single day of Heather's fight;

Todd & Michele, for providing us with sanity and good laughs over great games and company, even when the times didn't warrant it;

Mary and Jeff, for insisting we do the right thing at the very beginning and making the initial trip to Houston possible;

Todd, Nathan, Steve, Agustin, and Brad, for being the 'brigade' that helped Heather die in the way she deserved, and provided me with the companionship I needed to start recovering;

Jen, for always knowing how to make me smile and for being a good shoulder to cry on; and

Sara and Laurie, for helping me realize that a path to a new life existed, and then having the patience to help me find it.

Live. Love. Laugh.

Alex Gabbi

Austin, Texas 2014

thejourney@alexgabbi.com

I AM

CHAPTER 1

I am a different kind of survivor.

I am the husband left behind after cancer ravages and takes a wife before her time.

I am the father left behind to get up every day and make sure his three children never forget the wonderful woman their mother was.

I am the man who is thankful every day for the 20 years he had with the love of his life, but fears what the future will hold.

I am a different kind of survivor. But I am not alone.

This is a story of a family that fought through the ups and downs of cancer and that continues to persevere. This is a story of sadness, despair, and loneliness. This is also a story of hope, recovery and happiness. This is a story for every family that has been impacted by cancer. And it is a story for those families that fear that they may be one day.

This is the Heather Gabbi story. It is also the story of every mother who has fought with everything in her power and more to stay with her family. And it is the story of every family who finds a way to cope, remember, and persevere even after the battle is lost.

Because we are also survivors.

SI PER SEMPRE. PER SEMPRE SI.

CHAPTER 2

It was the autumn of 1993. I had moved to Austin from Italy a few years prior, where I had spent the vast majority of my life growing up. I was entering my last semester as an International Business major at the University of Texas at Austin. I was in that stage of my life common to young men in their early 20's – that perfect time when we are young enough to believe anything is possible, stupid enough to believe that we know everything, and arrogant enough to believe we are actually better than everyone else.

One of the final classes I needed to take to graduate was International Business Operations. The class contained a large component of case discussions so there was the opportunity to participate a lot, even though most people didn't take it. I almost immediately developed a crush on one of the girls in the class – a very cute blonde sorority girl.

But that was NOT the woman that almost immediately started getting on my nerves. She was also blonde. I wasn't attracted to her at all. In fact, she just consistently pissed me off from the other side of the room. Every single time we had a case discussion in class, it turned into an argument. I would say "black" and she would say "white". If I said "loud", she would say "soft". She seemed to thrive by trying to prove me wrong at every turn. In a class that was primarily quiet, she was the one that consistently called out what she believed to be my bullshit.

Her name was Heather.

I'm not quite sure exactly how things developed, but over the course of the semester, for both of us irritation turned into respect, and respect ultimately turned into friendship. A relationship that began on opposite sides of the classroom ultimately converged to the middle of the room.

She was unlike anyone I had ever met – it seemed that her life centered on having fun and especially learning about different cultures. Heather had just returned from spending a year in Spain. So when I met her she was definitely partial to all things Latin, and more specifically, Spanish. Maybe that is why we started becoming friends – as an Italian, her concept of fun was one that I could finally relate to. It was a very Latin concept of fun – one that involved friends, laughter, and dance as opposed to going out to get drunk.

Over the course of our final semester in school, we started spending more time together. For the first month or so that we started frequenting the same establishments, about half the time I spent out was waiting for Heather to show up well past her appointment time, a Latin trait she had picked up that I did NOT care for at all back then.

She never seemed to care. I would always be enraged by the time she showed up, sometimes hours late. But I always waited for the very simple reason that when she finally did show up, we would always end up having a great time, and so the frustration of waiting would quickly be overshadowed by laughter and fun.

Heather was independent. She was fun-loving. But I also found her to be a little strange.

About a week or two after our class dueling had been transformed into friendship, she asked me to go to a wedding as her date. In retrospect, I realize that this gesture meant nothing to Heather. She had only been looking to bring someone she had fun with to an event and nothing more. But at the time, I had been totally confused. I distinctly remember calling my best friend at the time and having the "what the heck" conversation – "What the heck does this girl want from me? Doesn't she realize I'm not interested in her like that at all?" So I called Heather back and told her that I wouldn't go. It is still a decision I regret to this day, and it may have been one of the last times I ever voluntarily chose to not be with her.

Over the Thanksgiving break of that year, Heather went skiing and I agreed to take care of her fish and cat while she was away. A pivotal thing happened that I believe changed the course of my life that Thanksgiving - Heather tore the ACL in her left knee. The strong caretaker instinct in me took over and as a result we starting really spending a lot of time together and getting much closer. I soon began to realize that I cared about her a great deal. Both of us decided that we would stay in Austin to look for a job after graduating. So we decided to share a condo along with another friend.

By December 17th, 1993, we had started dating. Just a few days after her December 28th knee surgery, we moved in together.

****

I have always been a person that is quick to make decisions, and even quicker to judge. Just a few weeks after Heather and I began dating, I already had a pretty good idea that she was the one for me. One evening, I can't even remember how, the conversation about kids came up. I still laugh today about Heather's stunned look when I nonchalantly changed a general comment about kids into a comment about "our kids". I knew back then that Heather and I would eventually have a family together. But after a mere few months of dating, Heather instead knew unequivocally at that point that she had moved in with a lunatic.

I was thinking about a future together. She was thinking about what we would do to have fun over the next week. I was thinking about my first of many get rich ideas (later in life I actually realized that getting rich requires hard work). She was thinking about how to make next month's rent. Very early on, Heather took the role of both cheerleader and conscience in our relationship.

About 6 months into dating and living together, I was absolutely positive that Heather was the one for me. After several failed relationships, including a heart-breaking long-term relationship in Rome shortly before I moved to the US, I was finally convinced that I had found the love of my life. I was ready to move to the next step. I began working in earnest to plan my engagement proposal. Just like everything I do to this day, as those that vacation with me can attest to, the engagement was to be impeccably organized - a complex confluence of many events - and special. More importantly, it was going to be a total surprise to Heather.

That proved to be a BIG mistake.

****

In retrospect, I wonder what on earth I was thinking. I did everything right in some ways – I asked Heather's parents for their approval of my proposal. I even organized surprise engagement parties in Dallas at Heather's aunt's house and in Sealy, Heather's home town in Texas, for a few weeks later.

With all the preparations complete, we loaded into the car and departed on the most important road trip of my life – to Memphis.

I had personally designed and had the engagement ring custom made from heirloom rubies and diamonds. In fact, the ring had been the first loan I had ever gotten approved for.

The plan was simple – propose to Heather in our Memphis hotel room at precisely 7 PM. I would have a hidden video camera so the moment could be recorded for posterity. And then about 20 minutes after the proposal, I would arrange for one of Heather's best friends, Julie, whom I had flown in from Nashville, to knock on the door and surprise Heather so that she could share the happy moment with one of her closest friends. After a few days of celebration, we would drive back to Dallas for a formal engagement party to share the big news with everyone.

Needless to say I learned some very important lessons about Heather that day. The most important of all was that she didn't just say it – Heather actually really did HATE surprises! Oops!

Hindsight is 20/20. In retrospect I laugh about so many things about the engagement:

1. Who the heck gets engaged in Memphis when they live in Texas?
2. Who proposes in a Best Western hotel room? On a strict schedule no less?
3. Who plans for a surprise engagement with someone who openly says they hate surprises? With no contingency plan no less?

But I couldn't help it. It had been my pattern my entire life. I was all in.

I learned a very hard lesson that day. I learned to become a student of human nature, because when someone's behavior is involved, you better have a contingency plan and assume things will not go as expected.

I would be far too easy on myself if I said that my proposal turned out to be an absolute fiasco. More than nine minutes after popping the question, begging and pleading, the best I could do was get Heather to accept the ring and tell me that at some point she might consider saying yes. Needless to say, the hidden camera video I took is footage that will never make it to prime time!

Little did I know back then in the hotel room that the wait time would not be counted in hours, days or months. It would be counted in years!

Without intending it, Heather had just taught me my second and third life lessons. Patience truly is a virtue. And good things really do come to those who wait.

* *

I have always been a true romantic at heart. Heather was always the pragmatist. Ironically, for one of the seminal events of our lives, the roles had been inverted. I had totally botched the wedding proposal by being way too pragmatic. On the other hand Heather, multiple years later, hit the acceptance out of the park by showing an incredibly romantic side that I didn't even know she had in her.

I found out later that Heather had been planning the acceptance event for multiple months. In fact, she had some good friends buy a gold bracelet in Florence during a visit to Italy. Heather had the bracelet engraved with a simple Italian phrase – "Si per sempre, per sempre si", which translates to "Yes forever, forever yes."

She chose a family vacation in Canada near Banff, during one of the many long hikes we took together during the course of our relationship, to surprise me with the acceptance. As romantic as the moment could and should have been, as with many other times in our relationship, the "acceptance" turned into a comical banter that many of our friends would tell you was always the main signature of our relationship.

Heather said "Close your eyes."

Of course, my immediate reaction was "No way, you want to put a frog or something else disgusting in my hands as a practical joke. I'm not falling for it."

Back and forth we went. Finally Heather, exasperated, said "Just close your eyes and put out your hand for God's sake!!!!" I acquiesced.

She dropped the bracelet into my hand. After a few stunned moments of silence, I realized my patience had paid off. I would finally get to marry the love of my life. My joy was immediate – I hugged her tighter and kissed her more passionately than I ever had before.

But of course there was a catch.

Heather's words sliced through the moment like a knife – "Wait. I will marry you. But there are several conditions."

Of course, I should have known better. After several years of our relationship being established, it should have come as no surprise to me that the proposal acceptance was late and came with conditions attached to it. Needless to say, the negotiations began almost immediately.

Heather began, "You have to quit smoking and learn how to two-step."

After a 20 minute raging debate, we settled on a compromise position – I would no longer be smoking by the time we got married, and I would take dance classes to learn how to two-step.

I remember being so proud of how clever I had been during the negotiation. My precise choice of words allowed me to exercise out clauses that almost made me wear my arm out patting myself on the back. I fulfilled my obligations – I completed a two-step class and had quit smoking by my wedding day.

But I exercised my out clauses almost immediately. I started smoking again on our honeymoon, mostly because the process of quitting had resulted in my gaining 60 pounds in the three months leading up to our wedding. And I chose to NEVER exercise my two-step skill. While I had committed to learning how to two-step, I had never actually committed to using my newfound skills in public. The thrill of victory for a while was infectious – I rarely won a negotiation or debate with Heather. In fact, I'm not sure I ever won another one.

A WONDERFUL LIFE
CHAPTER 3

One day many months after Heather died, my older son Nico asked me what had been the happiest day of my life. It proved to be a surprisingly difficult question to answer. In fact, Heather had always said we had a perfect life. And in a lot of ways it always had felt charmed.

We were married on May 2nd, 1998 at Green Pastures, a wonderful setting near downtown Austin, Texas. By many standards, our wedding was very small – just a little over 100 people. It certainly wasn't flashy.

Heather borrowed her wedding dress from one of her bridesmaids and our rehearsal dinner consisted of take-out BBQ in the backyard of our rental house. And after the wedding reception, our sole goal was to get back home and hang out with all of the friends that were staying with us that had travelled so far to come share the day with us.

In fact, our wedding day had just as international a flair as everything else we did. My groomsmen alone consisted of a Brooklyn Jew, an Italian, an Indian, and a couple of Americans.

I definitely won't pretend that our life was always perfect. At the time, my parents still lived in Italy. My father refused to attend the wedding in protest. He could not understand why his Italian son would marry an "ignorant" American from a small town in Texas. I will never forget his last words to Heather before he moved back to Italy – "good luck, you're going to need it."

Turns out he was flat wrong. It was only much later after my parents moved back to Austin and built a house on our property that my father finally appreciated who Heather was. In fact, they ultimately became very close.

Amazingly, it was Heather's big heart and willingness to always look for the positive that even made it possible for my parents to move back. How many wives would allow their in-laws to live right next door, especially after what had transpired with my father? This proved to be yet another reason she was so special.

I'd also be lying if I said we lived in marital bliss. Our life definitely wasn't perfect from that perspective either. If you put two strong-willed people into a relationship, you're bound to have conflict. It's not a coincidence that Heather and my banter and arguing became a signature of our relationship to outsiders looking in. But what made it all work was that we always shared the same set of core values and interests, and always were willing to compromise at the end of the day.

We always both thought that bucket lists were a ridiculous concept. One of the keys to happiness in both our minds was living life to its fullest every day. If you wanted to do something, go somewhere, or experience something, then the key was to stop thinking and start doing – always. We never fell prey to "this isn't a good time" or "we're broke" or pick your excuse inertia. Our philosophy was always that excuses and consequences should be damned. You could only ever truly say you were milking every ounce out of life if you were constantly striving to NOT have a bucket list. And that is exactly what we did.

The fact that our life had been so charmed was a source of great distress to Heather in her final weeks. She kept coming back to it – "our life was so perfect, this isn't supposed to be happening, not to us", she would say. I couldn't help but agree. I can only surmise that the karmic universe has a way of balancing – 20 years of perfection was bound to come to end at some point. It's just that I guess neither of us expected the 'balancing' to be so tragic and definitive.

So back to Nico's question – what was the happiest day of my life? I'm privileged to say that I have had many happiest days of my life. And I hope to have many more.

I believe that truly living life is about trying to make every day your happiest day. Just to name a few for me:

- The birth of each of my three kids
- Marrying Heather
- The day Heather agreed to marry me
- My first kiss
- Having my son trust me with a secret for the first time
- Seeing a stunning new place like the Sagrada Familia
- Having many wonderful meals
- Reuniting with long lost friends
- Thinking Heather's cancer had gone into remission
- Moving to the US from Italy

One of the big ways I try and honor Heather's memory daily is to try and strive to make each new day one of my happiest days. It doesn't always work, but it's about the trying. It's also about helping as many other people view the world in the same way. I often wonder how many happiest days I can help my children, my friends, and even complete strangers live. And that desire frequently is what has kept me going.

REVENUE PER MINUTE

CHAPTER 4

Right, wrong or indifferent, I have a long history with lots of different doctors as a result of three children, Heather's multiple reconstructive knee surgeries and her long bout with cancer. I feel privileged to have interacted with almost every one of them. Their job isn't easy. I think it's unfortunate that sometimes society brands doctors as greedy, overcompensated, egomaniacal and impersonal.

Most doctors labor through many years of medical school to exit into careers well after most college graduates, mired in debt. Then they work crazy hours and fight medical reimbursements on a daily basis to get paid for the services they provide.

Don't get me wrong – many doctors earn a great deal of money. But I believe they absolutely deserve it. Most of the doctors I was privileged to interact with, from our local pediatrician to the leading oncologist at one of the world's preeminent cancer centers, practiced medicine because they loved it and cared about the well-being of their patients.

But then there are the evil few. I don't choose the word "evil" lightly. These are the doctors that are truly just in it for the money. These are the doctors who choose wealth over wellness consistently. These are the doctors who practice paternalistic medicine, living in a past where the doctor's role is one of God and not partner in treatment. These are the evil few that give all other doctors a bad name and literally take lives into their own hands with no consultation, no discussion, no accountability and no justice.

I call them revenue per minute doctors. This isn't my term – this is their unpublished term, a sinister metric by which they measure the performance of their practice. This is a metric that by its very nature implies that patient volume should always supersede patient wellbeing.

This is the story of a revenue per minute gynecologist in our home town that may well have cost a loving mother of three and my wife her life. This is the story of their evil, greed, and denial until the very end.

****

We all know the type of doctor. They are the ones that you wait for hours past your appointment time to see, only to be greeted brusquely and ushered on your way after your five minutes in the sun. They are the kind of doctor that somehow presumes that their time is more valuable than their patients' time. They are the elite, the entitled. They are the doctors that play God while assuming their patients are all intellectually inferior morons, incapable of making the right decisions for themselves. They are the doctors that care more about money than they ever do about their patients. Always.

My story is about the one that may well have killed my wife. Were they holding the gun? Absolutely not. Did they pull the trigger? Absurd. But did they know there might have been a loaded gun pointed at Heather's temple? Most likely. And did they choose not to tell us about it? Most definitely.

Heather's OBGYN had come highly recommended by multiple friends when she had decided to switch doctors after Nico's birth. In fact, to this day they remain one of the most prominent OBGYN's in our community.

They did all the right things when they first took Heather into their practice. They took her family history. Heather's paternal aunt and grandmother had both died of cancer at a very young age – one of uterine and the other of breast. That had always been the source of Heather's fear of getting cancer. Based on this history, the OBGYN assessed Heather as high risk for breast cancer and agreed that she should get annual mammography beginning at the age of 30 and also recommended frequent self-examination. In effect, Heather was being treated as an at-risk patient.

We thought we were covered and were lulled into a false sense of security. After all, the OBGYN was reacting to her risk status. They were such smooth talkers that we actually believed they fully had our back. Even though it would be the last time we every blindly trusted a doctor, the decision to trust her OBGYN may likely have cost Heather her life.

When we received the initial diagnosis years later in the hospital room after Luca was born, I'll never forget the devastation they showed. They were holding back tears, saying that they were so sorry. It seemed so genuine at the time that I actually felt their pain. It was only later that my sympathy turned into anger. They were crocodile tears.

A few weeks into our fight with cancer, Heather and I found out about a hereditary cancer screening test that would have identified the genetic mutation that precipitated Heather's cancer. A positive result on the test would have presented us with several alternatives, including a full hysterectomy and double mastectomy, which would have lowered Heather's cancer risk back down to that of an average person. The shock to us was that her OBGYN had known about the existence of the test well before Heather's diagnosis. And even though they had clearly classified Heather as high risk based on her family history, they had never informed us of the existence of the test.

When Heather confronted them much later about this fact at a fundraising event, their response was so condescending it was sickening. They had intentionally <u>not</u> told us about the test. They didn't want to create unnecessary stress on us. Besides, they said, the test wasn't covered by insurance and cost several thousand dollars.

I can't relate to the personality type that takes people's lives into their own hands and makes life or death decisions on their behalf. The even more despicable thing is the power this doctor still has in the Austin community. To this day, they are still one of the most resistant doctors to hereditary cancer screening, even though now these tests are all covered by health insurance. When Heather and I contemplated pursuing legal action against him, the feedback we received from the legal community was quick and firm. This particular doctor was untouchable – they provided expert testimony to almost every major law firm in town, and thus pursuing them would be virtually impossible due to conflict of interest.

Heather showed such courage one afternoon just a few months before she passed away. The chemo infusion room at her oncologist's office overlooked her OBGYN's office. One day, just after receiving chemotherapy, she decided to go to them and set the record straight. And set the record straight she did, in front of the doctor's entire staff. She challenged them to defend their insistence to live in the past and ignore testing, and they still hung their hat on the test not being covered by insurance even though this was patently false. Heather made them a $100 bet that she would come back with all of the evidence that the test was covered by insurance. Unfortunately, she didn't live long enough after that to cash in.

For my part, I still can't find the courage or strength to take this to the finish line in her memory and go collect on the bet from the OBGYN. Maybe I'm afraid of what I would say if I did go their practice. Or perhaps I'm scared of the feelings that this would bring back up to the surface for me. Nevertheless, I'm not sure I will ever go see the doctor. I will however continue to do my best to tell their story of evil and paternalistic medicine in private to whoever will listen. And I do find peace in knowing that at some point they too will have their day of reckoning. At some point all of the times they make their patients wait for hours to be treated disrespectfully for 5 minutes, their false tears, their desire to play God, and even more sinisterly, their indirect role in the absence of a diagnosis, and perhaps even death, of who knows how many women with a hereditary cancer disposition due to lack of genetic testing, will catch up to them.

LUCKY LUCA

CHAPTER 5

It had been a raging debate for years. Heather came from a larger family of four children. I was an only child. You can imagine the discussions. I always wanted two kids – one of each – but would have been open to three had we not gotten a boy/girl combination on the first two. Heather always wanted a larger family.

Our compromise was a question of rounding – $(4+1)/2 = 2.5$. I always chose to round down to 2.0 after I got my boy/girl combination. Of course, Heather rounded up. And so every 3-4 months, as our friends called it, the great "rounding" debate would take place again.

One evening, in a moment of weakness or maybe temporary insanity, I acquiesced. We, or rather I, decided to take a chance once and let nature and/or destiny take their course. Of course, it proved to be a moment of incredibly poor judgment, since Heather and I would basically get pregnant by standing next to and looking at each other.

Regardless, I'd like to think that as with most marital battles, I would have ultimately lost this one anyway. Of course, in retrospect, this lapse of judgment probably got me an extra 2-3 years with Heather and most definitely got me one of the most wonderful children a father could ever wish for – Luca.

I remember getting the phone call while I was having a cigarette (yes, I still smoked at the time) in the garage of my company. My jaw hit the floor. "You're what?" I said, immediately followed by "Oh shit, I knew I shouldn't have rolled the dice."

We had a few difficult days with tough conversations. In retrospect, I still feel guilty for a lot of the things I even thought to bring up every time I look at the wonderful bundle of life and reminder of his mother that Luca is growing into.

Heather's pregnancy with Luca proved to be a very tough one. Unlike her pregnancies with Nico and Maya, Heather never really felt well during the entire time she was pregnant with Luca. We didn't really pay too much attention to it – every time we had an appointment everything checked out fine. We just both chalked up the pregnancy difficulties to the fact that she was much older – 39.

If the pregnancy was difficult, then labor and delivery proved to be even more so. We were in uncharted territory. Luca was one week overdue and so we went in for labor to be induced. This was the norm for us – Nico & Maya had been the same. But what turned out to be different was what happened once labor started.

Luca just wasn't coming out. In retrospect, I know that this was cancer related, but at the time it was Luca going into distress that finally prompted us into action. We agreed to an emergency C-section.

As I've said before, I feel privileged that I've been blessed with so many happiest days of my life. But the day Luca was born proved to be the most emotional day I've ever lived through. Frighteningly, the emotions had all been compressed into about 3 minutes in the operating room.

Joy. Seeing Luca be pulled out of Heather and placed on the scale and then realizing as with the other two kids that I was instantly in love.

Fear. Recognizing that Luca wasn't breathing and watching doctors and nurses scramble around him.

Relief. Hearing him cry and scream for the first time and knowing that everything would be OK.

Shock. Having the surgeon ask me whether Heather and I would ever want to have kids again as he held one of her incredibly enlarged, cancer-infested ovaries in his hand and requested to take it out.

Terror. As the understanding dawned on me that something was going terribly wrong. Heather had ovarian cancer, not the breast cancer we had feared and guarded against.

And ultimately, devastation. As I felt Heather's grip on my hand loosen and tears start streaming down her face.

****

After the initial shock of the diagnosis was behind us, the most important thing that came to our minds was whether and how we would tell our other two kids, who at the time were ages 7 and 9 – old enough to understand but not old enough to truly comprehend.

There were a few things that troubled us:

1) What should we tell the kids about their Mom's diagnosis?
2) What should we tell them about the prognosis? Specifically, did they need to know there was a possibility their Mom might die?

The most important thing of all to us was to ensure that no matter what, the kids didn't somehow associate Heather's cancer with our newborn Luca. There was no way we would allow that to happen.

As it turned out, we handled the first conversation the way we handled all subsequent conversations – by trusting in our children's intelligence and in their resilience. We decided to always be open and honest to them about everything.

[36]

We picked up both kids early from their elementary school on our drive home from the hospital. Of all places, we had our talk with them in the parking lot of a popular hamburger joint in Austin. The conversation was simple – we had decided to tell the kids that we would be giving Luca the nickname "Lucky".

We specifically picked the name Lucky to emphasize the fact that not only was Luca not responsible for Heather's cancer, but that he actually had helped save her life by allowing us to find it. We stressed with the children that Luca's part of the battle was helping us find the cancer but now that it was up to us to continue the fight. We told them to the best of our ability what the process would look like (we were far from the experts we would ultimately become at that point) and asked if they had any questions.

Nico, the oldest, as was typical of him even at so young of an age, got right to the point. He asked "Are you going to die?"

It was our first opportunity to deviate from our goal of honesty, but we stayed the course. We told Nico there was a chance his mother would die, but that we were going to do everything in our power to ensure that didn't happen.

On the other hand, Maya's reaction was the humorous response of a 7-year old who didn't fully grasp the magnitude of the conversation at the time, but who for sure understood that she was now stuck in the middle between two male siblings. Heather and I giggled at her comment, which showed so much perception and intelligence in a radically different way. Her statement was also simple and to the point in its own very special way: "Since Luca's work is done now, can we give him up for adoption?"

The rest of the car conversation proved to be as uneventful as you could imagine given the circumstances. The kids started asking a lot of questions, and we realized that we didn't have nearly enough answers. Foreboding what was to come, it was remarkable how quickly the kids adjusted to the shocking news. It still never ceases to amaze me how resilient children can be and how frequently we as adults underestimate them.

One thing that the car conversation drove home for sure was that Heather and I couldn't do it alone. We began gathering the help we needed and started where it was most important – our kids. It was at that time that one of the most important organizations that we came to lean on entered our lives – Wonders & Worries.

WONDERS & WORRIES

CHAPTER 6

There aren't a whole lot of times in life when someone or something special appears that is most unexpected and that sticks forever. For me, the introduction to Wonders & Worries (W&W) (www.wondersandworries.org) was just that.

W&W is an incredible organization dedicated to helping children cope with the serious illness of a loved one. They fill such an important gap. Just as this book is about the survivors that are left behind, a category of people that I believe to be underserved by organizations and literature that is currently out there is children – not the sick ones, the healthy ones that are one day faced with the reality of potentially watching one of their parents die. W&W addresses the needs of those children.

When Heather was first diagnosed, we knew almost immediately that we would be very public about our fight, that we would lean on whoever would offer us help, and that most importantly, we would always be honest and open with the kids about the situation, the process, and their feelings. But beyond knowing what we wanted to do at a philosophical level, we really had no clue how to actually implement these desires.

That is where W&W stepped in for us. In the early stages of Heather's fight, they provided a foundation for Nico and Maya to realize they were not alone. There were other kids just like them going through the process and there was strength in numbers. This emotional support proved to be most pivotal to Maya, who was 7 at the time of initial diagnosis and very emotionally fragile.

Nico on the other hand had always been the more rational and pragmatic child. W&W appealed to him by demystifying the treatment process. I'll never forget Nico's reaction to visiting a chemotherapy infusion room, seeing an MRI/CT machine, and understanding the treatment process in terminology he could relate to (he was 9 at the time). In general, people are most frightened of the unknown and I believe this to be especially true of children. W&W eliminated the unknown for Nico.

Even though they still realized their Mom could very well lose her fight with cancer and die, for Maya knowing that other kids like her were in the same situation calmed her down tremendously. And for Nico, understanding what was going to happen not only through our discussions with him but also the formal talks and field trips by W&W served to allow him to move on with his life.

As Luca grew, he too was provided with an emotional outlet to deal with his grief. Maya continued to meet one-on-one with a W&W social worker for the entire duration of Heather's treatment and beyond. They provided her with the emotional outlet that she needed to begin to heal.

Even though W&W has no services for adults, they proved to be just as therapeutic to me. During Heather's fight, they were the organization that we could both get behind because we had directly realized the benefits of their service. We considered ourselves so fortunate to be in Austin because W&W was here.

In later conversations I had with the W&W Executive Director, I frequently wondered why no other cities other than Austin would have something like them. There were children everywhere who had sick parents that needed help understanding and coping. I always remember being stunned when representatives of W&W would describe a rejection for funding from some company or another with the excuse that the organization couldn't relate to the cause. What company however large or small hasn't ever had an employee or family member affected by cancer? And what did the employee's kids do? I honestly couldn't think of a broader, more emotionally important cause.

Heather and I decided that we would do what we could to help. We concluded that we should cater to our strength – hosting parties – and determined that once a year we would host an event at our house to raise money for W&W.

In subsequent years, this has become somewhat of a tradition, with an annual event being hosted on Memorial Day weekend. I'm proud to say we've donated well over $25,000 to date to the cause and I am personally constantly looking for ways to do more.

I have a more active role in the organization today than ever before and am grateful for the opportunity to serve. It has helped me so much in the healing process to know that I'm raising money for an important organization with an incredible cause. And it feels good to know that the money I am helping raise has a direct impact on children's lives in Austin. My dream one day would be to help there be a W&W in every major city in the US and have my event and other activities be some of the most significant sources of funding for them.

It is no coincidence that W&W will receive a significant amount of the proceeds from the sale of this book. They deserve it. They need it. And they most definitely have earned it.

They have already left an indelible mark on my family that will never be forgotten.

HOPE IS NOT A STRATEGY

CHAPTER 7

The first visit to any oncology medical practice must always be shocking for people. It definitely was for Heather and me. Over time you numb to it, but the emotions the first time are overwhelming when you walk into a practice or specialized hospital and see just how many sick people there are; how many people cancer is indiscriminately impacting.

However, the part that was even more saddening to Heather and I was always how many people's eyes were glassy and empty. They were going through the motions. They were dead people walking. I've read many times that the human instinct to survive is one of the strongest we have. But I have to say that in cancer it is one extreme or the other, and it is 50/50 at best. Either people are like Heather and fight until the bitter end, or they give up quickly and fade away. I haven't seen much in between. Whether it was because they didn't have a support system, or they had simply given up, it was always stunning to both Heather and I to see how many people were just going through the motions instead of taking control of their own lives.

Doctors are human. As with all humans, they are not infallible, nor are they able to think of everything. We were privileged to have had a medical team that had the self-confidence to listen to our opinions, the patience to let us know when we were being stupid, and the courage to tell us when we had a great idea that they hadn't thought of.

Heather always had a great analogy that described our approach to her medical care. She called it the "treatment bus". The treatment bus represented the universe of things and people that would combine to form our treatment regimen. Our job was to find people and options to join us on the bus – the more people on the bus the better. You never wanted an empty bus. But at the same time, we would never forget that we were the driver of the bus – the rest were passengers with opinions.

Even though we didn't win our battle with cancer, Heather and I were both proud of the way we staffed our treatment bus. Chemotherapy has a way of messing with your brain – your deductive reasoning and your memory. Heather recognized this early and really began to lean on me more and more to be the bus driver, while offering opinions and discussing key options with me.

All of Heather's doctors cared tremendously about her and her treatment – she had managed to touch them as she had so many other people. But no matter how empathetic they were, I figured they could never possible care as much as we did. For them, it was their job. For us it was our lives.

So we made a commitment to one another to never become passive. And I took it upon myself to become an absolute expert in all things related to the treatment. I was so obsessed that some of my friends in the medical profession jokingly began saying that I should be offered an honorary MD, albeit my knowledge was about 1 millimeter wide and 10 miles deep.

First I became an expert. In ovarian cancer. In the BRCA gene. In nutrition. In chemotherapy agents – both mainstream and experimental. In treatment protocols. In side effects and their management. In alternative therapies. In human psychology. And in record management, from symptoms to therapies to medical conditions. I became so good that there ultimately were several situations where I made a correct diagnosis or suggestion before a member of our medical team arrived at the same conclusion.

In the process of becoming an expert, Heather and I frequently discussed how we should get people on our bus. It proved to be a combination of Heather's charm, the persistence of our friends, and my analytical

[45]

approach and growing expertise that allowed us to recruit the best possible team for the bus.

We had some of the best oncologists, nutritionists, alternative medicine professionals and friends on the bus. We took ownership of our treatment plan and never relinquished it until the very end. That made all the difference in so many ways. After the fact, several people that were in charge of treatment told us that they were hoping to get Heather to survive 12 months. She lived for 38 months after her diagnosis.

Not only do I believe that our approach to her treatment allowed her to live longer, but I also know in my heart that it allowed Heather to have a much higher quality of life. Even as we were entering our final days, it allowed us to have the peace of mind that we had done everything right. We had no regrets. There was nothing we could have done better.

Even now, over a year after her death, I still grieve and miss her daily. But our management of the treatment bus has freed me from the guilt and uncertainty of wondering whether Heather would still be alive if I had done something different.

Ironically, we were precariously close to never even knowing the treatment bus existed. We had pressure from friends, family, and even Heather's OBGYN to not seek the best. When we brought up MD Anderson in Houston, the vast majority of the responses we got were

"Don't go", "Houston is too far, you can just get everything in Austin", "You're just a number there", "It's all about quality of life". We heard this so much that we almost gave in without even knowing what we were giving up.

Then a friend named Mary stepped up. She didn't even live in Austin. But she was a nurse. Mary knew that the bus needed to be filled with as many quality passengers as possible. So she contacted MD Anderson without our knowledge. She made us an appointment with the preeminent expert in ovarian cancer. And she forced us to go in the nicest possible way. In effect, she had shown us that there was a bus, handed us the keys, and identified our first key passenger.

Our visit to MD Anderson was devastating and eye-opening. We realized how many sick people there were in the world. But at the same time, we realized that while other people's opinions were important, we had to be the ones in charge. Had it not been for Mary, we probably would have listened to our support network and never gone to Houston.

An executive at one of my customers always said that "hope is not a strategy". As a result of my experience with the treatment bus, I can truly say that there is no truer statement. People can go through life "hoping for the best", but good things happen to people that make the best happen and actively seek it out.

If you know a loved one who is impacted by cancer, please take it upon yourself to be their "Mary". Do not let them hope for the best. Allow them to be optimistic. But at the same time, hand them the keys to the treatment bus and tell them to drive. And if they don't have a license, then drive it for them. Don't let a doctor drive the bus. And please don't let them leave the bus in the parking lot.

LEAN ON ME

CHAPTER 8

Right after her diagnosis, Heather and I were blessed to get the advice of two women – a caregiver and an ovarian cancer survivor – that fundamentally altered our initial approach to seeking help. Getting a cancer diagnosis and having to deal with all of the initial treatment decisions and emotions can be difficult enough. But for us, injecting a newborn (in addition to two other young kids) born by C-section and immediate chemotherapy needs into the equation proved to be completely overwhelming.

When Heather and I finally got to go home from the hospital with Luca, we honestly didn't know how we would be able to keep it together, even with my parents living next door and helping. We were very fortunate to get advice at the time from two wonderful women. Other than showing us the ropes around treatment, the caregiver provided me with some incredibly insightful information around a topic that I least expected – managing help.

In hindsight, I realize just how much her advice helped me and how spot on it was. In a nutshell, here is what she said:

- Lots of people will want to help – accept the help but direct it! Accepting the help made us realize that you needed an army to help with the fight and that it was OK to be public about your needs. It's amazing how many people view it as a sign of weakness to ask for help. I have come to view asking for help as a sign of strength – to be honest about your situation and have the courage to admit you can't do it alone.

- Manage the process using a schedule or a web site. If you don't take a proactive approach to organizing people's desire to volunteer help, regardless of motive, then you will end up with a million flowers you don't want, or tens of meals that you throw in the garbage because you are getting them all at the same time. With her help, we identified a web service that allowed us in less than 24 hours to set up a calendar for people to schedule their volunteerism, a request list, and an avenue to provide updates to everyone so I didn't have to tell the same story dozens of times. This web site proved to be a real life saver for me.

- She also made me realize that there were different kinds of people that would want to participate in the process. It took me a long time to realize that none of these roles were good or bad, but rather all necessary and beneficial as part of the process. She identified the different categories of people for me:
    o "Regular Friends" – friends that wanted to help however they could but that needed to be prodded and that within 90 days or so would need get back to their own complicated lives
    o "Obligated Friends" – people that wanted to do something just to feel good about themselves without really spending time on the process
    o "Business Friends" – people in the professional network that needed to do something to check a box
    o "Long-Term Friends and Family" – people who you would consider to be the closest to you that would always be there for you

Her point was to leverage different groups at different times. As counterintuitive as it was at the time, her suggestion was to ignore our instincts and push our close family and friends away. She suggested we look at each group as having a "shelf life". Obligated and business friends wanted to do what they could with money but

[51]

limited effort for the shortest amount of time. They were out to do the right thing, check the box, and feel good about themselves. She suggested to make it as easy as possible for them to help out and leverage the group for as long as possible. For us it was about getting food delivered and a nanny paid to help Heather with Luca while I worked. We ended getting about 90-120 days out our first group of people for meals and nanny.

Then we moved on to regular friends. These were the people that genuinely wanted to help by doing things for us. They would help whenever asked but didn't want to impose. At the same time their personal lives would sometimes get in the way. This became the group of people that would accompany Heather to chemotherapy, bring a meal by once in a while, and help us shuttle kids around. They lasted until Heather's first extremely brief remission, after which they assumed everything would be OK and got back to their normal lives.

As an aside, it's interesting to me how few people that haven't directly been affected by it underestimate the impact and ramifications of a cancer diagnosis.

When it's all said and done what remains is your closest friends and family. They are the ones that won't have taken personally that you have somewhat ignored them while capitalizing on other's desire to help. They are the ones that have patiently waited their turn. And they are the ones that take over after everyone else runs out and stick with you to the end.

These were the people that effectively lived with us the last 7 weeks of Heather's life. They were the ones that took turns cuddling with her in bed and letting her talk. They were the ones that watched her slowly fade away. And they were the ones that refused to allow me to see her body removed from our house, opting instead to place the emotional burden upon themselves to spare me and the kids the memory.

FIREWORKS

CHAPTER 9

I will never forget the day we sat in our local oncologist's office and came to the conclusion we were out of options – that there was nothing left we could do. Heather's body was breaking down. Her cancer was spreading. It had become clear that she would no longer be able to tolerate any treatment, assuming that there even were any new alternatives available.

Heather had an uncanny ability to bond people to herself. I'm honestly not sure how it happened, but it just did. People she had known for brief moments in time became inexorably tied to her in one way or another. Even our Austin oncologist was unable to hold back their tears when they confirmed that we had arrived at the right conclusion and that there was no longer anything to be done.

I can't even begin to imagine what this truly felt like from Heather's perspective, but I can unequivocally say as her closest friend and confidante that the actual decision to die is equally as devastating if not more so than the process itself.

Later that day, I made the mistake of asking Heather how we planned on telling the kids that we were "giving up" the battle. I immediately regretted my word choice after I said it. Even though she was already weak and emotionally distraught, Heather jumped into my case with the usual fervor and intensity so characteristic of our relationship.

"I am NOT giving up" she said forcefully. "I will continue to fight to live until the very last breath. And that is what the kids will see. I will die with as much dignity and passion as I have done everything else in my life. And that is also what the kids will see. That is ALL they will see. Do you understand?" I nodded. She had been crystal clear.

Even in her last 7 weeks of life, Heather taught me more about what it means to live, love and laugh than I had learned on my own in a lifetime. When we went home that afternoon, Heather had 100% blockage – in other words, she couldn't eat food or absorb fluids without throwing them back up. It was May 25th. I so hoped that we would be able to celebrate one more of her birthdays together on June 10th.

Once again, I underestimated her. Heather did not die until July 4th, after almost 7 weeks of complete starvation piled on top of an already depleted, sick, ravaged body.

[56]

It seemed only appropriate given who she was as a person that she would die on Independence Day.

The hardest thing I have ever done in my life was to watch her die. Her will didn't break until the very last few days. Incredibly, she managed to even fill our last days together with more laughter than tears, more good memories than bad, more life than death.

The last weeks were an emotional roller coaster, filled with joy, laughter, sadness, anger, confusion, and much more.

Even in her last weeks of life, Heather refused to stop enjoying the finer things. I remember her defiantly saying that just because she couldn't swallow food or drink anymore didn't mean she couldn't enjoy its taste.

And so the infamous spit cup came into existence. It was a ridiculously oversized coffee mug that Heather used to spit out her food since she couldn't swallow anything. She enjoyed every single gourmet meal we cooked and savored every flavor before spitting her food out into the cup. We laughed so hard – it was typical Heather. Stare a horrible situation down and stubbornly refuse to let the situation win and get the upper hand. It was like she said "Screw you bowel obstruction, I'm still enjoying my food. I win!"

Every day she would find peace in enjoying a swim with family and friends. She would literally float in the pool for hours. When she became too weak to get down the stairs, I built a ramp so I could roll her down in a wheelchair. When she became too weak to get in the pool on her own, I carried her in. She swam up until the very last few days of her life.

Every day she would hold court in our bedroom. Close friends would come through to say their goodbyes. Instead of making it sad, Heather would find ways to reminisce happily about times past. She would both find and provide comfort to the people she saw. As the days went by, I found myself becoming more possessive of her time, but at the same time more uncomfortable that I was monopolizing it.

I watched almost in tears as my father said goodbye in the only way he knew how. He played his violin for her. He played music that moved the heart – works that I had never heard him play for anyone else. He had come so far from misjudging a country girl over a decade earlier. The music he made spoke a message that came across loud and clear to Heather – "I love you" – words that he had never spoken to anyone including me but were heard clear as day on that day.

Heather's brother would finally introduce the family to the girlfriend that he had kept under wraps for months. And Heather would give him the approval that he wanted. She was a good woman that would treat him right after a disastrous first marriage.

Only her father let her down, as he had so many other times in her life. In her moment of greatest need, he simply did not show up. His rationale was that he simply couldn't bear to see her in her deteriorating state. I was furious – it was such an act of unilateral selfishness. I was offended. It was like he assumed we were happy to see her in the state. No one liked seeing such a strong woman slowly deteriorate. But we were there because she needed us. And I was devastated. I had considered it a personal failure on my part to not be able to ensure that her father was there for her in Heather's time of greatest need.

Many months later, after little to no communication, I finally had the courage to confront him over the Christmas holiday. I had made peace with myself. I told him that for the longest time I harbored anger toward him for abandoning my wife and his daughter. But then one day it just occurred to me that he had to live with himself for doing that to her, and that would be far worse than anything I could do to him. And so I forgave him.

****

In her down time when people weren't around, Heather and I talked about our memories together. I watched her try her best to get caught up on all her photo albums. She also made memory boxes for each of the children and for me. She cried as she showed me what was in each of the children's memory boxes – the photo album chronicling her life, her recommended readings, a small teddy bear, and an individualized letter among other things.

Then she apologized. Even though she made me promise to not look in my box until she had passed away, she told me that my box didn't contain a letter. Heather said she had thought about it for a long time but realized that there was nothing left to say. In a way, that was what made our relationship so special. We never left things unsaid. When there was an argument to be had, we had it. When there was a place to go see, we went to see it. And when there was an act of kindness or passion to be had, we had it.

When I did open my box it didn't contain a new letter. Instead, what it did contain was every letter that we had ever written each other. I had no idea Heather had kept all of them. I remember sobbing uncontrollably as I reread each letter – it is almost as if she had known that would be the first emotional release I would have. There was also a teddy bear to keep me company while I slept, her photo album, her most special piece of lingerie, and other items. As always, she had chosen exactly the right things she knew I would need to keep.

****

Even in her final weeks, the altruism that so made Heather the person she was in life also defined her in

[60]

death. She was obsessed with making sure that I would be taken care of. I have only since scratched the surface on the sheer number of promises she had friends make – they all had a specific task that involved watching out for me and/or the kids.

She tried multiple times to have THE conversation with me. She was so concerned that I wouldn't meet someone else and try and move on after she died. She kept trying to make me commit to moving on. She even tried to suggest people.

It proved to be the only time in our relationship we were unable to have a conversation about something. But I just couldn't do it. I couldn't. And I don't regret it.

THE SPEECH

CHAPTER 10

After Heather's diagnosis, one of the things she almost immediately got incredibly passionate about was hereditary cancer. Through a friend of a friend, she was introduced to a company named Myriad – the inventor of the genetic screening test that could well have saved Heather's life had her OBGYN informed us of its existence.

Myriad has historically always had very strong patient advocacy groups – a collection of survivors, previvors, fighters, and believers in the hereditary cancer cause that band together to help spread the word to doctors, medical establishments and the general population. As a result of her sales background, her passion on the issue, and her direct personal experience, Heather was the perfect candidate to become a patient advocate for Myriad. In order to become an official advocate, she would need to complete a multi-day workshop in Salt Lake City, Utah at Myriad headquarters.

Unfortunately, Heather's dream to become active in the hereditary cancer advocacy movement never came to fruition. Every time she got her workshop scheduled, something would happen. She would hit a bad patch from a treatment perspective. Or we would discover a new metastasis that needed immediate attention.

The closest she ever got to attending a workshop involved actually making it to Salt Lake City. We had decided to spend the weekend there together before she started her workshop on Monday.

We knew that Heather potentially had a tumor that had grown back but fully expected it to be localized and just require radiation. I'll never forget the horrible moment – the phone call – from our Austin oncologist.

We were in a movie theater at the Salt Lake City Temple learning about the history of Mormonism. Heather took the call. After not seeing her return for 5 minutes, I ventured out into the hall to look for her.

She was crying so hard she was heaving. Heather simply did not cry – it was completely contrary to her nature. I could only assume that the news had been devastating. And in fact, it had. It was the Fall of 2013. And it was probably the last time until the end in 2014 that Heather would truly feel like herself. The cancer had spread much more than we had expected. In retrospect, I look at that moment in Salt Lake as the beginning of the end of the war. After receiving the news, we took the last hike in the mountains that we would ever take as a couple.

After Heather passed away, I resolved that I would continue to try and fulfill her dream of advocacy in her stead.

Thanks to the foresight of one of the local Austin Myriad employees, I was given the opportunity much earlier than expected. Less than a week after Heather's passing, the local employee that had originally reached out to Heather approached me and asked if I would consider being the keynote speaker at Myriad's sales conference in Las Vegas. The catch was that the conference was the following week, less than 10 days after Heather's death. I was torn. I wanted to do it, but at the same time I wasn't sure if I could emotionally handle it so soon.

As Heather and I had often done in the past, I consulted with the kids and asked their opinion. They all thought it was a good idea. Maya even said she wanted to come. So we booked tickets to Las Vegas. One of Heather's closest friends offered to join us so that Maya wouldn't have to be alone in the crowd during the speech. I will always have a profound admiration for the bravery that Maya showed to come listen to the speech on that day.

As awkward as I find myself being in a lot of social situations, standing in front of a room with hundreds of people is not one of those types of situations. In fact, under normal circumstances I would say that it fell directly into my comfort zone.

But this event was special. It was so soon after Heather's death that I was an emotional basket case. I felt all the pressure in the world to succeed. To me, delivering the speech of my life would honor Heather's legacy more than anything else in the world I could do. I knew how important this would be to her. There was no way I would let myself screw it up.

So I did what I absolutely never do when I give a speech – I wrote it down word for word. I wanted to make sure that every word was perfect. I wanted to minimize the chances that I would simply break down on stage and not be able to continue.

The speech primarily consisted of two letters – one written from Heather's perspective and one from mine. Below is the complete transcript of the 15 minute speech that began my transformation and slow healing process.

****

Dear Myriad,

My name is Heather Gabbi. I wish I could be with you today in person to talk to you about the importance of what you do and how much I believe in your cause. I tried multiple times to get involved with you but unfortunately my illness always seemed to get in the way.

I died peacefully in my home on Independence Day.   For 38 months I fought my ovarian cancer with no reprieve, no breaks and no remission. I withstood multiple surgeries and hospital visits, 3 different cycles of radiation, several bowel obstructions, 9 rounds of Carboplatinum and Taxol, 5 rounds of maintenance Taxol, 5 rounds of Gemzar and Cisplatin, 5 rounds of Doxil, 4 rounds of weekly Taxol, 1 round of Topotecan and 7 weeks of total starvation before I finally succumbed. My husband and I always joked that each year we would set a record for when we hit our insurance out of pocket maximum – our personal best was January 3rd. Please know that I am proud of the fight I put forth even though I ultimately lost – it was easy. I had so, so much to live for.

I am not only proud of the fight, but I am proud of how I did it. I never let cancer have the upper hand. I tackled every day with the joy, love, curiosity and passion of a child. In the three years I fought cancer, I traveled with my family to Italy, France, England, British Columbia, New York, Quebec, Seattle, and Utah. I built retaining walls, a soccer field and a wood-fired pizza oven on our land for my family to enjoy. I took up and became an accomplished mosaic artist, decorating multiple areas of our home with my newfound skill. I taught Spanish at my daughter's elementary school, imparting many other children with the passion for languages, travel and cultures I have always cherished. And I continued to be the best mother and wife I could. I even found time to dispose of a rattlesnake when I got home after my first day of chemo! Even though I had to give up my high-tech sales career, I found as many other ways to make an impact, live, love and laugh as I could. And I have no regrets. You see, life to me was always about laughter and smiles, never sickness and sadness. Even the memorial I personally planned for myself was a Celebration of Life. I am happy to say that at my memorial party over 500 adults and children smiled and laughed in celebration of life, eating home-made pizzas, enjoying cotton candy, diving on slip 'n slides and making snow cones all the while making many new happy memories in the Texas heat.

In this letter, I want to tell you my story, in hopes that it will bring you the faith and strength to continue to do what you do. I do this because my story is important, and it needs to be told.

I grew up in the shadow of my family history. By the time I was in my twenties and was old enough to care and understand, I lived with the certainty that one day I would get cancer. Two women in my father's lineage died young of breast cancer and ovarian cancer respectively, so I constantly carried with me, right below the surface, the knowledge that I too someday would likely have to fight the disease. At that time, I discussed my family history in detail with my gynecologist, a very well-respected doctor in the Austin community. He *agreed that my history placed me at significantly higher risk and as a result recommended that I start breast cancer screening at the age of 30 just to be safe. I thought I had covered my bases, having read that early detection would be key when that point in time came that I would ultimately have to fight the fight.*

My doctor and I were on the same side. I TRUSTED him. Over the course of time, he helped me give birth to my children. He had been an integral part of some of the happiest moments of my life.

And then came the fateful day – the day where tears of both joy and grief were spilled simultaneously – May 8th, 2010. My third pregnancy had been really tough. But I had chalked it up to age; I was 39. After many hours of labor, I was making no progress, and my baby was going into distress.

My husband and I made the decision to move forward with a C-section. After some terrifying moments that seemed like an eternity when the doctors couldn't get Luca to breathe, I heard the baby cries that every mother waits for to sigh in relief. But when I heard the doctor ask my husband whether we were ever planning to have any other kids, saw the look of fear in his eyes, and heard him say "take it out", I knew something was terribly wrong. The next 10 days were a complete blur – receiving the stage IIIc ovarian cancer diagnosis, dealing with the shock, starting my recovery from the C-section, breast-

feeding my baby for the few days I could before starting chemo, telling my kids for the first time that I might die, and after much cajoling from some key friends, agreeing to go for a consult to MD Anderson, even after my local gynecologist, the doctor I still blindly trusted, repeatedly advised me against it.

I will never forget my first visit to MD Anderson. It was during that visit that one of their genetic counselors met with me. After about the first 15 minutes of hearing my family history, the conversation proceeded like this:

"Have you been tested for the BRCA mutation?" she asked.

"I'm not sure I know what you mean." I replied.

"With your family history I'm 100% positive you have the BRCA mutation. We should get you tested just the same but I'm telling you right now you have the mutation. Are you telling me your doctor in Austin never told you about the test?" I could tell she was stunned.

By the end of the meeting, so was I. The doctor I trusted, that had been seeing me for years, that had helped me bring two children into the world, that knew my history and had assessed me as high risk already by having me get frequent mammograms, hadn't told me about a key fact. There was a test that could tell me that I had a dramatically increased chance of getting breast and ovarian cancer; a test that would give me the freedom to choose to take action before I contracted the disease. I refused to believe this was true.

When I returned to Austin I confronted him. I will never forget his condescending tone as he told me that the test really wasn't appropriate to recommend in any situation and that furthermore it cost multiple thousand dollars and wasn't covered by insurance. In an instant my world crumbled – the medical professional I trusted the most had withheld key information from me. He had stripped me of my freedom and right as a patient to be informed and make my own decisions. He had made assumptions about my financial situation and ability to afford the test. In short, he had played God. I didn't know what to say – the need to fight for my life quickly took center stage and the betrayal slowly faded into the back of my mind.

At the beginning of this year, I started my new chemo regimen at a new location. As fate would have it, the infusion room overlooked the parking lot of my gynecologist's office. With no hesitation I knew what needed to be done. I had some unfinished business with him – I needed closure. After receiving my round of Taxol, I walked across the street to his office accompanied by one of my good friends and most reliable chemo buddy. I take great pride in the fact that I had the courage to confront him in front of his whole staff, armed with 3 additional years of knowledge of Myriad, genetic testing, and the BRCA mutation. And yet in spite of the preponderance of evidence and very personal case study I offered him, his arrogance still prevailed. He fell back on the excuse of insurance coverage and would still not agree to introduce testing into his office where applicable, citing that it wouldn't be appropriate for most people so why create the stress and panic at all. I finally got him to agree to a $100 bet – he would pay me the sum when I returned to his office with a list of all of the insurance companies that would pay for a Myriad BRCA test.

Sadly, shortly after the confrontation my health really started to deteriorate. I was able to pull together some of the data we bet on but was never able to cash in on the $100. One of my final requests of my husband was that he collect on the bet. I would like for you to help him do so. And I would like for you to use my story to help break down the barriers of both ignorance and arrogance that other gynecologists you sell to may have. I would like you to restore the right of all patients to understand the facts and risks associated with their genes and provide them with the freedom to choose their own destiny.

Love & Hugs,

Heather Gabbi

****

Dear Myriad,

My name is Alex Gabbi. I am the proud father of three wonderful children – Nico, Maya, and Luca. I am a successful sales executive for a Fortune 150 technology company. I am a well-respected professor at the McCombs School of Business at the University of Texas at Austin. And as of July 4th, I am also a widower.

I keep telling myself that I am one of the luckiest men alive. I got what most people spend a lifetime looking for – I found the love of my life and was able to spend almost 20 years with her. And yet I don't feel lucky. I feel alone, empty and lost. When I'm not sure what to do about something, I find no answers. Because my best friend and confidante is gone. When I'm in need of a hug and kiss to make everything alright, my arms and lips find only empty space. Because my lover is gone. When my children need their mother, I can't give her to them. Because she is gone. When I need a smile to light up my heart, soul and a room, I can only find it in pictures. Because my wife and the love of my life is dead. She is gone. She is never coming back.

Not a single minute goes by every day that I don't think of her. And so many times the same questions haunt me. I unequivocally know, like her, that we fought the best fight we could given the circumstances we were presented with. We did everything right post-diagnosis. We just lost.

But the questions still haunt me – the "what if" questions that I'm sure you're thinking of right now too:

What if we had been empowered with the knowledge of the BRCA mutation and the risks it entailed?

What if we had known about the Myriad test and taken action based on the results?

What if a well-reputed gynecologist in Austin hadn't practiced paternalistic medicine but rather given Heather and me the freedom to choose our destiny?

What if we had been treated with the respect that all patients deserve? The right to have all of the facts and make our own medical decisions?

What if that same well-known gynecologist had accountability for their actions, or in this case, inaction? What if they feared repercussions for their arrogance?

Then I take a step back and realize that anger is not what Heather would want me to feel. I convince myself that outrage at a doctor playing God is not what is required for me to heal. And so I persevere. I try and make it through every day with a smile. Today I still have to pretend it is ok, but I allow myself to hope that maybe someday the pretending will stop and it will start actually being ok.

As I continue to search for what will give my life meaning going forward, I know one thing for sure. I owe it to the memory of my wife to tackle life with her passion, perseverance and enthusiasm in everything I do. And my request of you is that you do the same - at home, at play, and at work.

Sincerely,

Alex Gabbi

****

I would like to leave you with a few final thoughts. Look up now – look at the family picture on the screen. Study it carefully.

I want you to see a 12-year old named Nico who will never get to have his mother see his next soccer game or the man he grows up to be. And I want you to know that one of you could change that for another family. Because what you do matters.

I want you to see a 3-year old named Luca who will remember that his Mommy makes him happy, because that is what he repeats every day, even though he may not actually be sure why that is the case. I want you to see a boy who will never know his mother, even though he is her incarnate. Then know that you have the power to change that for another family. Because what you do matters.

Now look at me, and see a broken man searching for a way to be fixed. I am a father trying to find a way to be good enough to raise his children in a way that would make their mother proud. I am a professional trying to find new meaning in jobs that feel so trivial now. I am a man hoping that 20 years of joyful memories will carry me through the balance of a lifetime of loneliness. Look at me and please come to the conclusion that in your trade failure should NEVER be an option. Because what you do is built on the foundation of what is morally good and right. Because what you do saves lives. Because what you do matters.

And finally, I want you to see a beautiful 9-year old little girl named Maya. I want you to see a child who will never get to share her secrets, her love, her successes and her children with more than a 5-page letter from her mother. I want you to find her in the audience, because she is here today to give me strength, and I want you to tell her that her mother didn't die for nothing. I want you to tell her that the next time a doctor tries to blow you off, you will fight for her in memory of her mother so that you can help the next Maya. I want you to tell her that you will not take no for an answer from anyone. Ever. Because what you do matters.

In Heather's name, please leave this meeting and make it a personal mission in what you do day in and day out to find, save and preserve the next Gabbi family. When you have doubts, find strength in Heather's story. Find strength in my story. Find strength in the knowledge that what you do matters.

On behalf of the Gabbi family, thank you from the bottom of my heart for inviting me here today to tell our story. It was an honor and a privilege. And more importantly, thank you from the bottom of my heart for the job you do and the fight you fight. From sales professional to sales professional, I leave you with one final word: WIN. Thank you.

****

Honestly, I had been terrified about the impact that traveling to Las Vegas and reading the speech would have on me. Right after I accepted, I wondered if it really was too soon for me to take on something of that magnitude. I was unsure whether I would be able to keep it together enough to deliver the results that Myriad was looking for in addition to helping my own cause.

But candidly, delivering the speech proved to be exactly what I needed at the time emotionally. As an added bonus, it began a relationship with the only other company other than W&W that continues to play a huge role in my life to this day – Myriad.

With every word that I read to the audience of several hundred salespeople, the darkness that had clouded my mind since Heather's death cleared a little bit. By the end of the speech, I wasn't sure how exactly I would ever feel better and be able to deal with Heather's loss, but I unequivocally knew that I could find new purpose in life and that the new purpose could keep me going.

The final tipping point for me occurred right after the speech. I had gotten a standing ovation and moved people to tears. But that wasn't it. It was person after person coming up to me telling me that they would not let Heather down. They would tell me that they would use our family picture as motivation every day to drive them to never give up.

This was a sales organization for whom one primary form of evaluation was the number of lives they saved per month. A really poor performer indirectly saved over a dozen lives per month, which seemed more significant to me than any sales deal I had ever closed. Their *worst* performers were saving over 12 lives per month!

After the crowd dissipated, a Myriad executive approached me and said something I will never forget. They are words that continue to drive me to this day. He said "In 15 minutes you probably just saved over a thousand lives." I instantly knew that even though I could never bring Heather back, the prospect of being able to help keep other family units intact could be a worthwhile cause to keep me going in the dark hours I was sure to face in the months ahead.

And keep me going it did. With uncanny timing, every time I would start spiraling into depression or darkness, I would get an e-mail from a Myriad salesperson telling me about how they had used my speech for motivation to finally get through to a tough doctor. That would be all I would need to get myself up and keep going.

Saving lives was something I could truly get behind. But at the same time, the experience in Las Vegas also help me realize that I would need to change other aspects of my life. All of a sudden, when compared to saving lives, high-tech sales, my career for the last 9 years, seemed quite trivial.

CELEBRATION OF LIFE

CHAPTER 11

I had writers block for almost 20 years. It is ironic that the first legitimate piece of writing I did that truly broke the block would be Heather's eulogy. Perhaps it was meant to be that way. Since my most precious gift had been taken away from me, as a balance I was given back a forgotten gift that would equip me with an outlet that could help me deal with the loss.

One of the last things that Heather and I discussed and planned together was her Celebration of Life. Heather adamantly refused to have a funeral. Instead, she wanted a party at our house where friends, colleagues, and children could gather together to have fun and laugh with one another. One of her final wishes was that people not be sad at her passing, but rather make lots of new joyful memories in her name.

Kids had always been a key part of our lives. On any given day, our home swarmed with them. Our friends didn't understand why we always had such a commotion at our house. To me it had always been clear. Children shared Heather's curiosity and joy for life more closely than many of the adults we passed our time with.

Heather's Celebration of Life was anchored by a "Passport to Fun". Children and adults alike were encouraged to move through a wide variety of fun stations such as slip 'n slides, cotton candy, popcorn, and a dunk booth. Each time they completed a station they would receive a stamp in their "Passport". Completed passports were turned in and one random winner would receive a $1000 check. The only requirement in receiving the check was to use the funds to travel somewhere in the world you hadn't been before and then be prepared to tell the story the following year. A classmate of Nico's from middle school won and chose to go to Costa Rica. She told her story the following year, when a new couple won the prize and traveled to Belize. I hope the tradition continues forever as it is a way for Heather to impart her curiosity for travel onto others every year that may otherwise choose not to have the experience.

Just as I would script my speech to Myriad the following week, I thought carefully about the message I wanted to deliver at Heather's Celebration of Life. It was very important to me to get it right. And I knew I would be emotional.

Ultimately, these are the words that I read to a crowd of gatherers of well over 500 at sunset on the day of

Heather's Celebration of Life, right after a moment of silence when we released hundreds of butterflies into the air in Heather's memory:

For those of you not from Austin, at a place on Lake Travis called The Oasis a bell is rung to bring in the sunset, with the hope of stopping the hustle and bustle just long enough to appreciate what nature can give us all on its own. It seemed only fitting to me that this would be the time for me to say a few words to you all.

This sculpture [a small girl with arms widespread standing on top of the world set on a pedestal in the middle of a fountain] was our last major purchase, the perfect capstone for the courtyard garden paradise that Heather built around us. Heather named the sculpture Gabi, because Gabriela had always been one of her favorite names but we realized pretty early on that naming a child Gabi Gabbi would just be downright cruel. The artist, Angela de la Vega, named the sculpture "Joyful Empowerment", and to be candid those are two pretty good words that I would use to describe Heather. But to me, this sculpture was, is, and always will be "Heather".

In this statue I will be reminded daily of the things that mattered most to Heather and do my best to continue to keep them alive and well at our house in and in our community.

Welcoming new learning opportunities, a new family or new travel experience with open arms.

Meeting all challenges with the joy and smile that only an individual with a child's heart and curiosity can have.

Making her children, me or even a person she met 5 minutes before feel like they were on top of the world.

I have thought long and hard about what I could possibly say today that would do Heather's life justice, and I have failed. As I requested, many of you have shared wonderful memory letters to our children about what their mother meant to you. The best I can do for you and for Heather today is share my letter to the kids with you.

****

Dear Nico, Maya & Luca,

What broke your mother's heart the most was writing the long letters she gave to you in your memory boxes. I didn't get a letter from her – she told me there was nothing left to say or do between us and I totally agreed. You see, that was the single greatest gift your mother gave to me. She taught me every day to do everything I could to remove the "un" from my life.

She was the master at it. Don't leave a good question unasked or unanswered. Or an opportunity for a healthy debate untaken. Don't leave a place unexplored or a stone unturned. Don't leave anyone in this world unloved or unhugged. Don't ever make anyone feel unappreciated. Don't leave a task undone. Don't leave something unsaid that should be said. I could go on and on.

But if you focus on removing the 'un' from your life every single day, then you will truly have lived life to its fullest. And you won't have anything left to say or do either. This was your mother's gift to me, and the gift I will do my best to pass on to you.

I have tried so hard to put in words what your mother means to me. And what I discovered is that she already put in words what I want to say way better than I ever could have. So instead of writing something myself, I will leave you with her words as my words, especially since I know it would make her laugh to know she was getting in the last word after all!

This is from a letter she wrote to me from Sealy on December 25th, 1993, just one week after she and I started dating almost 20 years ago:

"As I sit here thinking of you and how good and happy you make me feel I think of two things – how lucky I am to be so close to you and how I empty I feel without you here. When we are together I think I am the happiest person alive. You have given me the ease to entirely be myself. You know just what to say, or not to say, to make me smile. It is next to impossible to imagine life without you - to never have your smiling face brighten my day or *your loving way support me. Everything that happens in some way reminds me of you, and I want to share it with you. We are going to make great memories in our new place. And with mutual respect, communication and trust these memories will be special ones I will never forget."*

To each of my children from Mommy I say "Te quiero, te amo, te adoro."

To my lovely Heather I say "Amore mio, si per sempre, e per sempre si."

And to all of you I say thank you – keep the smiles and laughter going.

The celebration exceeded all of my expectations. Children were children all day – laughing, running and playing. Even adults allowed themselves to become children again for a brief moment in time. It was exactly what Heather would have wanted. I felt her everywhere. It made me smile.

MEMORIES

CHAPTER 12

Shortly after Heather got diagnosed with cancer, a wonderful woman briefly came into our lives. She had been fighting ovarian cancer for over a year and was our first introduction into how tight-knit a group the survivor club really is. We didn't know her at all, yet she wanted to do everything she could to help. She provided us with tips on how to manage our treatment, track side effects, curtail chemotherapy side effects, and overall how to manage the disease. Her name was Ella, may she rest in peace.

After Ella lost her courageous battle against cancer, one of the things her family did to memorialize her was ask everyone to submit memories of her in the form of letters to her children. I distinctly remember Heather and me discussing what a wonderful tribute that would be. As our children grew, if Heather did lose her battle, we thought it would be amazing for them to keep the memory of their mother alive and live up to her legacy not just through their memories or my memories, but also the stories of the many people she had touched over the course of her life. We thought that the sheer number of extra perspectives would be irreplaceable.

As it turned out, for someone like Heather, whose charisma touched anyone she came across, the stories poured in by the dozens along with never before seen pictures. The end result was over 200 type-written pages of memories and dozens of pictures for me and the kids to cherish for the rest of our lives.

For some reason, reading and transcribing those stories was a daunting task. I tried several times over the months that followed her death and simply could not get past the first couple of memories before breaking down. Even one year later, when I finally was able to make it through all of the memories, edit and transcribe them, by the end of the process I was a teary, depressed mess. It took me days to recover my footing.

I combined all of the stories and pictures into an album. One day, I'm not sure when, I will print a copy for each of the children and place it in their memory boxes for them to read when they are ready.

What follows are some excerpts of the tales of Heather's wonderful life from the eyes of those who were around her at different times. My hope is that in providing these I am able to harness some of Heather's positive energy to touch each of my readers and empower you to change something about your life for the better, no matter how big or small.

****

"Wherever I went with her she made it fun!!! She really made me happy at all times and she always made me smile. She was so generous to everybody and changed my life forever. I always loved to see her. She will always be in our memories."

– Elementary School Student

"I learned from Heather. She did not just look at her children, she took in everything they did into her heart and soul. This experience made me change the way I talk and listen to my children. I am grateful for this lesson she taught me."

– Fellow Mother

"Just as your mom made the choice to do everything she could to live, I hope you will also choose to do everything you can do to live, make a difference in the world, and make the most of your life, not only to celebrate your mom's memory, but also to honor yourself."

– Fellow Cancer Patient

"Upon meeting her, I instantly loved her. She was so welcoming, fun and positive. She made you want to stick around and chat a while and she always made those around her feel so important. Heather was one of a kind. I cannot tell you what a special place she holds in my heart and how much she has shaped my life over the past few years. She always put life into perspective for me. Against all odds, she fought hard and NEVER complained to us. She would wake up each day and fight and live life to the fullest. She was an inspiration to me. I learned 3 things from your mom and I know you have been given these gifts as well. Number 1 was WORK HARD. Heather always had a project going on and the challenge was never too big or too small. She got out there and got her hands dirty and was determined to accomplish her goals. Number 2 was GIVE BACK. She gave countless time and energy to her charities and volunteered wherever she was needed. She put other's needs even before her own. She was willing to go door to door, even though I know she was not feeling well, and collect used items for the families she was supporting in Mexico. She never had self-pity and thought of others during her greatest time of need. Number 3 was LIVE LIFE TO THE FULLEST. I learned to do things that I wanted to do and not worry about the little things. She would say, "Who cares". If you want to do that, then do it. Who cares what anybody else thinks. We deserve happiness. She had wisdom even beyond her years. I learned to wake up every day and say, "Life is good". She

gave me perspective. If I were ever having a "bad day" or a challenge in my life, all I had to do was think of Heather. That would change my whole attitude. Heather had the biggest challenge of her life for the past 3 years, yet she woke up every day and lived life to the fullest."

 - Friend

"She was open and loving and always up to opening up to welcoming a new friend. That was perhaps one of her most amazing qualities, her uncanny ability to make a friend in 5 seconds flat and make the person feel as if they were the most important human being in the planet. I will always remember this as one of her incredible qualities and I hope I can live my life closer to this mantra."

 - Friend

"Where do I start with Heather? My husband and I live next door. Heather was a neighbor, a friend, a teacher, an artist, the life of the party, someone the world really couldn't afford to lose, but lost anyway. "

 – Friend & Neighbor

 "She said once that she did not have a bucket list – that she had lived her life to the fullest. I think she wishes very

much that you have fun, that you love hard and deeply and that you give back as a citizen of the world while you explore every single castle and beach in the world. Of all of the people that I have met thru my life, she has been the one that taught me that loving deeply means showing it deeply at every turn."

- Friend

"There are people you will meet in life who are "sources of energy". They make you think, make you laugh, ease your worries, inspire you and bring a smile to your face - Heather was one of them."

- Friend

"Each school year begins as a blank slate, and over time a unique picture of learning, laughter, tears, and hugs begins to emerge. Every class has special moments that continue to live with us long after third grade memories fade. This year your mom was our bright shining star. From our first Spanish lesson, she held us spellbound. Her energy and enthusiasm was contagious. Our lessons were made up of so much more than vocabulary and tricky pronunciations. Never afraid to follow a path that might take us to Italy or Pakistan, your mom always made everyone excited to be a part of the journey. She opened our hearts to embrace the joy of our world, the

wonder of unknown cultures, and the promise of new places to be explored. Your mom was a treasure who gave unselfishly. I know you will grow up still surrounded by her indomitable spirit. Her memories will always be reflected in the countless ways she made a difference by sharing her strength, her determination, and her awe of the beauty of the world."

- Elementary School Teacher

"We all die. But we all don't live as well as she did. We are very proud to have known Heather and the Gabbi family. They have faced loss with grace and a determination to "live, love, laugh."

– Neighbor and Friend

"Well, it took me entirely too long to figure it out, but it finally occurred to me that Heather, my friend, and EVERYONE'S friend, just didn't care to make a big thing out of HER life events. She did not waste time or money on things that she thought were selfish or unimportant. For her and your dad, it was more important to spend money helping out a friend, buying a car so someone could have a better chance at a job and school, or throwing together a dinner of whatever pasta they had in the house and somehow making it taste great to anyone who happened to be there! Your Mom and

Dad had it figured out from the beginning - friendship, adventure, and personal growth are what it's all about!"

— Friend and Bridesmaid

"I was only a kid, but she spent so much time with me...made me laugh, taught me new things, and generally, it was always fun to be with her. I now realize how much I looked up to her, and the more time I spent with her, the more she began to be my role model, someone I would want to be like when I grew up: always with a smile, full of friends, good with everybody, active and adventurous... a genuine, fun, outgoing person, loved by everybody."

- Friend

"I appreciate learning from her that crazy ideas are important, and it is even more important to try to make them real."

- Friend

"Thank you for having taught me that our body can be gone but that our spirit is truly immortal. Thank you for also proving to me that being stubborn, spirited, independent, opinionated, nosy, loud and constantly on

the move are traits that we should all value. I have often heard that true wealth is not measured by the size of a wallet, house or bank account but measured by the impact you have on loved ones and people around you and your community. This impact is like a print you leave on someone, or place. She left a huge print. Everywhere I look in her house or outside, I see her. I feel her. I look at Maya and hear and feel her strong personality, I look at Nico and I see her gentle and kind heart, and when I look at Luca, I hear and feel her energy and spirit."

- Friend

"Here's the thing: your Mom had an incredibly special gift of being able to help others believe in themselves, reach beyond what they'd previously accomplished or dreamed, go farther and do more than they'd ever believed they could. Her gift fell on fertile ground when it came to me. She challenged and inspired me to do things which, quite literally, changed the course of my entire life."

– Friend & Bridesmaid

"She reminded me constantly (by her actions - not her words) that life was always about enjoying and living for the moment, the best way you could, and helping others. Every time you look up in the sky, I believe the number of

stars you see represents the number of positive things your mother did for others."

 - Friend

"Heather is one of the craziest, fun people I have ever known. She loved entertaining and having loads of kids at the house ALL the time. ☺ She was also one of the most caring people I have ever met. As you are growing up and new opportunities arise (even if they seem a bit scary) I want you to think about your mom and know that inside each of you is her strength and go for it! She would want you to try as many things as possible. And remember not to take life too seriously. She didn't, and that's a gift she has given you. Your mom lived enough for five lifetimes. Now it is your turn to follow in her footsteps."

 - Friend

"I think of Heather and I think of a phrase from the Old Testament that you may be thinking about also: "A Woman of Valor." Have you read this one? 'A woman of valor… she opens her hand to the poor and reaches out to the needy… she is robed in strength and dignity and she smiles at the future… her children rise up and call her blessed, her husband, also, and he praises her… give her the fruit of her labor and let her achievements praise her at the gates.' (Proverbs 31: 10-31) There is some nuance and substance in the original in Hebrew that I want to share with you. "A Woman of Valor" comes from this phrase in Hebrew -- אשת חיל ("Eshet Hayil") -- and there is more than one way to understand that. In Modern Hebrew, חיל ("Hayil") is the word for "soldier," actually, so when we think of valor here, and the kind of valor that Heather had, let's think of bravery, courage, and a real warrior... beyond a virtuous person, Heather was a courageous person, a fighter for what's right, a fighter for her friends and her family. You can see those things in her, can't you? You'll be able to see them in yourselves, too, I have no doubt."

 - Friend

"I first met your mom in 2000 when I first arrived in Austin. From day one I realized that your mom was unique in a good way. She was genuine, refreshingly honest and transparent. She truly cared for others, and never met a stranger. She had a love for life, adventure, friendships, and family. She never hesitated to put others before herself, and she loved to share family stories (especially of you, she was so proud of you)."

 - Friend

I remember going to Yosemite with you and your family. I recall a group of us wanted to hike Mist Trail and Glacier Point. Several wanted to keep a quicker pace, but I could not keep up. Your mom stayed back with me like the good friend she was. Your mom and I spent several hours together enjoying nature's beauty, taking pictures of each other, talking about family, sharing thoughts and building memories. To this day, that trip holds a special place in my heart because your mom made it special."

- Friend

"I just wanted to let you know that Heather made such an impression on me when we first moved here. She was the first person to greet me and welcome me to the neighborhood while I was walking my dog. It's never easy being new, and people like Heather make big transitions a joy. It's easy to stay in your shell but so much more rewarding to reach out and make others feel loved. I love people who teach others this through their actions."

- Friend

"She was always curious and ready to strike up a conversation with anyone interesting. She had a real passion for life and lived it to the fullest."

- Friend

"When I think of her I think of a smiling, intelligent, curious, active, generous person. She loved life in all its aspects. She had feeling for every living species, flowers, animals, people, and I see how much she loved you guys. It was so natural for her to bring happiness around."

- Friend

"As smart as she was, she was not one to hold on to the information but willing to share and teach others."

- Friend

"I wish to let you know, that when we made the move to Austin in September 2008, your mother was the very first to invite us to her home. Knowing no one, she made time to entertain us, and introduce us to friends and family."

- Friend

"The way she gave herself out to people without expecting nothing in return is something I never met again in my life and I'll always remember her for that."

- Friend

"My friendship with your mom helped make me who I am today. She taught me so many things...how to enjoy the moment, how to be myself no matter what, how to enjoy Texas gardening, that hard work can be fun, or never be afraid to tackle anything, and to let children be themselves. Her smile and "can-do" attitude brightened many of my days and taught me so much about life and myself."

- Friend

"I was fortunate to be part of a large but exclusive group that could call Heather my friend. I started thinking, "What is the 'one' word that best describes Heather Gabbi?" It was hard to imagine picking one single string of letters to describe someone like Heather. In fact, it's not fair to burden any 'one' word with such a large task that captures everything she was & meant to her family and friends. But, listening to stories and drawing on my own experience I came up with the 'one' word I would pick. The word was genuine. She was a genuine friend. I remember getting a text from Heather at 5:30 AM seeing if I could put in a good word for a friend of hers that was looking for a job. It wasn't odd that she was thinking of how to help a friend or that it was so early in the AM. It was that she was texting me with this request while she was preparing to go into surgery after her cancer was discovered. She was the most genuine mom. She loved

her kids and has left her imprint on all of them. She was a genuine wife. She adored Alex. The passionate banter between them was always priceless."

- Friend

"She was the one who taught me that dreams don't happen on their own and that you have to give them a chance to come true. I guess she made me realize that if I wanted more out of life, I would have to do more than just dream about it.

Thirty years later I have traveled to over 27 countries, had countless foreign adventures and am the first in my family to not only attend college, but earn a master's degree as well. As I write this letter and look back to my early conversations with your mother, I'm amazed at what a difference she has made in my life. I will always be grateful for her vision and friendship."

- Friend

"When I gather rocks to build a wall and put the stones into place, when I put just the right tile into a mosaic and dream big plans for enchanted gardens, when I catch a hint of fragrance from sweet almond trees on a summer breeze-- trying to figure out just what it reminds me of-- I will think wistfully of Heather and travel to the place of recognition."

— Friend and Teacher

"I never saw your mom compromise her beliefs."

- Friend

"One of the things that always impressed me about your mom was how giving she was. Throughout her life your mom did things for people just to make them happy. She was kind and thoughtful and could always make me laugh and smile. I was standing on a stool the other day and realized your mom had sent it to me 15 years ago just because she knew I would like it. It's shaped like a giraffe, and I love it."

- Friend

"Your mom was one of the most curious people I've ever known. You'd tell her something and she'd ask you 10 questions about it, just to know more and dive into the details. She asked me questions about my life that I'd not even thought to ask myself."

- Friend

"It wasn't enough for her to see something – she had to get up close and touch, smell, taste. Your mom knew how to experience life, not just walk through it. "

- Friend

"Last I talked with her was almost exactly a year ago. She had texted me a "have a nice weekend" at midnight PDT. She couldn't sleep and mentioned the recurrence. Alex, I would have given her a kidney or a lung, but could not give her what she needed except for the most heartfelt love. Yesterday, I texted her phone, one year to the day. Nico answered. Please show him this email."

– Former Co-Worker

CANISTERS OF ASHES

CHAPTER 13

A few days before our first Christmas without Heather my son Nico asked me a simple question. I will never forget the avalanche of emotion his apparently innocuous statement elicited.

"Nobody has asked you what you want for Christmas, Dad. So what do you want?" he asked.

My response at the time was genuine: "I want for you kids to have a good Christmas." It felt right enough at the time, so much so that I even posted it on Facebook. Looking back, I'm pretty sure that Nico, Maya and Luca had as good a Christmas as can be expected for a first Christmas without your mother. In retrospect, I'm really happy that I didn't expose the other feelings that I was having at the time the question was posed.

I did honestly want my kids to have the best Christmas ever, and my credit cards will attest to the fact that I tried really hard! But no amount of money could change the outcome for me. No matter how much I tried, for me the same thought keep seeping into my consciousness.

"Canisters of ashes."

When Heather passed away, we had some of her ashes distributed into 100 tiny little canisters with the intent of placing each one in places old and new that we thought Heather would like over a lifetime of family travels - places as naturally beautiful as Mount Rainier and as simply fun as Schlitterbahn, a large water park in Texas. The canisters became part of our family fabric almost instantly, so much so that in heart-breaking fashion Luca, our three-year old, began referring to them as "Little Mommies" and kissing them before we buried them on location.

As my children opened present after present on Christmas, with genuine smiles that little by little warmed my heart, a big part of me still remained empty. I slowly realized that this empty part was only fillable with the 93 remaining Little Mommies, and no amount of children smiling could make it right.

Canisters of ashes. As other husbands kissed their wives that holiday season, I was left to continue to contemplate a future of travel, family, and life without Heather. I was left to think about a lifetime without her smile, her thrill for adventure, and her love of all things new.

Little Mommies. As other children hugged their mothers that holiday season, my children were left to smile without Heather and to make new holiday memories without her laugh or traditional yummy Christmas breakfast.

****

So much time is spent thinking about how to ensure that a lost loved one isn't forgotten. There are dozens of volumes written on different techniques you can use to keep their memory alive. But honestly, while I think that this is important, I have come to the conclusion that it is just as crucial to weave the loved one into the fabric of the family by allowing for NEW memories to be made with them. For us, this goal has been brought to life with Little Mommies.

Heather loved to travel almost more than anything else. By bringing Little Mommies with us on all of our trips, it gives our family the opportunity to talk about Heather when we are having the most fun, while at the same time making new memories that incorporate her into our fabric. These memories are then preserved for posterity. In fact, we have a small canvas of the best picture taken from each Little Mommy location, with time and date, hung in our stairwell. It is filling up quickly, and my hope is that one day there will be no room left to hang anything, and moreover, nothing new that we think Heather would have loved to see.

Little Mommies are our way of keeping Heather interwoven on a daily basis into the fabric of our family. I think everyone should do this – it creates an opportunity to make new happy memories with the loved one rather than having to search into a deeper and deeper past to find them, something that can be increasingly complicated for children to do as they grow up.

THE TREE OF LIFE

CHAPTER 14

Heather was one of the most physically strong people I have ever met. Her idea of a good time was working in the yard, landscaping, and probably most of all, moving huge limestone rocks by hand to build retaining walls all over our property. She dreamed one day of our home's landscape being on the Parade of Homes.

But during treatments, and especially as time progressed, it became harder and harder for her to work in the yard alone. So she enlisted the help of others. Just as importantly, instead of feeling sorry for herself, she sought new experiences. One day, one of her girlfriends invited her to go to a mosaic class. Within weeks, a new passion was born.

Mosaic art proved to be something that Heather carried with her throughout her cancer treatment. It appealed to her analytical side while also fulfilling her artistic side. It was relaxing. And she was good at it. I for one am thrilled she developed a passion for a physical art as I am gifted with the opportunity to view her works around the house with a smile every day.

She was most interested in mandalas, highly symmetric geometric mosaics that are stunningly beautiful. I think that one of the reasons that she gravitated to them is because of their strong Moorish influence, which reminded her of all of the happy experiences she had while living in Seville, Spain for a year during college.

Unfortunately, Heather never got to see her most ambitious mandala project completed – the Tree of Life. She had been collecting magazine clippings, sketching designs, and brainstorming on the project for months. When it became clear to her that she would never be able to finish it, in the final few weeks of her life she enlisted the help of her mosaic instructor and friend to realize the project.

Her design was spectacular and captured the essence of what Heather wanted while at the same time providing an amazing emotional twist. The tree would be viewed from the top. The main trunk would be represented by a miniature version of Heather's best mandala, which had been modeled after one of the mosaics in Ravenna, Italy. It would represent Heather at the heart of her friends and family. Four red hearts would represent our family. Gold branches would emanate from the core trunk to represent her impact on her friends and family. The leaves on the branches would be miniature mandalas.

The instructor's stroke of genius was to invite Heather's friends and family to her studio to each make one of the mandala leaves, so that in a sense they would be touched by Heather one last time but also be with her and our family for posterity in the work of art. The Tree of Life represents one of the most emotionally charged works that I have ever seen because of this.

When I want to feel at peace, think about Heather or recall the strong network of friends and family she had that loved her so dearly, I go in our garden and sit by the Tree of Life. In the words of the mosaic instructor:

"She asked me to help create her Tree of Life Mandala down near the pizza oven. I am very happy to be able to have helped create this work of art for your family. It is a mosaic that is in memory of your mother, and also for each of you. The Tree of Life is symbolic, and the design for this mosaic was created by your mother. My job was to make it happen. She collected all the materials, and described to me what she wanted it to look like. She envisioned a beautiful work of art, and I hope you all will enjoy it for many, many years. Many people wanted to help with it, so I figured out a way for everyone who wanted to help to be able to create a part of it, even if they didn't know how to make a mosaic. As a tribute to your mother, I am creating the center of the mosaic in honor of her. It will be just like the center of the mosaic on your house. My hope is when you see it, you will have

good memories of the special person she was, and the great love she had for all of you."

– Mosaic Artist

It is not coincidence that of all of the places I could have chosen to place a canister of Heather's ashes on our land, she lies under the Tree of Life, directly aligned with the main trunk and hearts.

THE JOB INTERVIEW

CHAPTER 15

During the entire time Heather was sick, as well as the five years prior, I worked as a senior manager for a large semiconductor distribution company. At one point, I took one of many trips to the company's headquarters. As part of the trip, my boss at the time wanted me to meet with one of the senior leaders of the company. What I expected to be a quick get to know you session turned into a multi-hour, unexpected job interview.

During this time I was asked a profound question, which unbeknownst to me at the time would come to shape the way I would deal with my future. The question was "What do you want your legacy to be?"

I thought it was one of the most difficult questions that someone had ever asked me. For sure, it was a question that was really hard to answer truthfully and not with a standard canned interview response. I told him just that initially. But as I thought I would need to just start talking and buy myself time until I could come up with something, the answer hit me clear as day.

I had honestly never thought about my legacy before I had been asked the question. This interview occurred before Heather's cancer diagnosis, and legacy just wasn't a question that "young people" were supposed to discuss. It was something for the old.

I now understand that legacy is something that everyone should think of at any age. It is also something that should be revisited occasionally, as an individual's answer could probably change over time. For me, the act of answering the question provided a clarity of purpose and pure guiding principle for my life that I had never formally had before.

My response was "I want to make a difference for people in their lives." It was simple. It was pure. And it was honestly what made me happy. Just verbalizing the phrase opened the flood gates for me. I began elaborating and providing him with example after example for what seemed like forever.

In work, I wanted my employees to feel that I had their interests at heart. I wanted to feel like I was helping them be more successful, and more importantly, I wanted them to feel like I was helping fulfill their career aspirations, whatever those might be.

At home, I wanted my kids to feel like their lives were enriched because I was in them. I wanted to help them grow into the adults they wanted to be. I wanted them to be successful in whatever way they defined success. I wanted to help them be smarter, more fulfilled, happier, and better human beings.

In marriage, I'd like to think that Heather and I made each other better. I learned more from Heather about how to appreciate life, place value in all people, and find laughter everywhere than I could ever describe in words. And I truly believe that Heather developed an appreciation for the finer things - food, art, architecture to name a few – because of me. She had the foundation but I build upon it significantly.

More than anywhere, I feel my need to leave a legacy when I set foot in a classroom. That is probably why I adore teaching. If even one student every semester said, years later, "that Alex guy – he made a difference for me", I would truly be fulfilled.

The clarity that the interview provided has never left me. I truly believe that it helped make my coping with Heather's death a little less devastating. This was because at my very core I knew what I needed to do. I knew and was able to articulate the very essence of what drove me. Ultimately, all I needed to do was act on it.

YOU WILL NEVER BE THE SAME

CHAPTER 16

On Saturday, May 24th, 2014 I hosted the 2nd Annual Heather Gabbi Celebration of Life. The theme was Roman, particularly fitting since I am from Rome and Heather's favorite monument was the Pantheon in Rome. Every time we went to Europe, we would always take a picture in front of the Pantheon.

Looking back over the year following Heather's death, my first week back at my job in October, 2013 proved to be extremely pivotal for me. During a business trip to Denver, I saw a large group of people that I hadn't seen in a while at our annual sales conference. Almost every conversation I had went exactly the same way. "How are you doing?", "It's good to have you back", and "Sorry for your loss" were the common themes.

I honestly didn't know how to respond. The truth wouldn't have worked: "I'm not doing well. I miss the most important person in the world to me. I'm not sure what to do next. I'm angry that her death may have been prevented if her OBGYN had genetically screened her. I'm devastated that I failed at the most important task of my life – keeping my wife alive."

As I struggled with these thoughts, something completely unexpected happened. Someone I hardly knew approached me and said something that ended up having a profound impact on me. Coupled with the impact that speaking to the Myriad sales team had on me in July and the mark the job interview had left on me years prior, this person's words proved to be the final catalyst to change the course of my personal history. Their words were simple and from the heart, and in retrospect, exactly what I needed to hear at that time. They said: "Today is the second anniversary of my son's suicide. All I can tell you is that over time you will start to feel better than you do right now. But no matter what you will never be the same."

They were right. In that instant I knew that I would need to change things up. I had to stop going to work to a job that was a constant reminder of what my life was like, no matter how wonderful those memories were. Indeed, it was then that it became clear to me that no matter what I did, I couldn't bring Heather back or ever have that life again.

Instead, what I needed to do to truly begin healing was honor Heather's memory. Many ways to accomplish this were immediately clear to me – help expose kids to global cultures and languages, teach more, get back to my roots and start a new business, and travel with my family and spread more Little Mommies. In a lot of ways it became obvious to me that in essence I needed to pursue my desire to leave a legacy – the notion that had come out of my job interview multiple years prior.

But today nothing plays a more crucial role in my mind in honoring Heather's memory than the "cause". One key part of the cause is helping other children cope with the serious illness and/or loss of their parent. I do this through the support of the organization that helped our kids through the process – Wonders & Worries. They were the annual beneficiary of the Heather Gabbi Celebration of Life. Myriad represents the other key part of the cause and are stewards of a crucial responsibility in honoring Heather's memory.

THE BUCK STOPS HERE

CHAPTER 17

If someone told you that you had an over 80% chance of getting breast cancer and an almost 50% chance of getting ovarian cancer would you be scared? If that same person told you there was a simple, nonintrusive test available that could tell you whether you had those odds or the odds of the general population (<10% and <2% respectively), would you take the test? If you took the test and it did come back positive, but you were told you could reduce your odds back to normal levels by having a partial hysterectomy and double mastectomy, would you?

Even though Heather's family history strongly indicated the presence of a genetic mutation like the BRCA gene (since made famous by actress Angelina Jolie), these were questions that she never had the opportunity to ask or answer because of her OBGYN. Yet the test in question exists. And it has existed for years. In fact, the test has even be covered by insurance in many cases for several years. The original breakthroughs in this testing arena were made by a company named Myriad, the very same company that had invited me to speak at their sales conference in Las Vegas shortly after Heather's death. Myriad is also the company that Heather had so wished she had been able to represent to doctors like hers as a patient advocate.

****

Since Heather's death, I can say I've taken on quite a few causes. But none of them is more important than to talk to anyone that will listen about hereditary cancer and the BRCA genetic mutation.

There are so many people out there that don't have a chance. Indeed, for so many victims cancer is truly an indiscriminate killer. But there are also so many people out there that could be empowered to change their own personal history. The only thing preventing it is ignorance in the truest definition of the word.

Whether it's because at risk patients with family history that would be strong candidates for testing trust their doctors to inform them and give them the best care possible. Or it's because someone chooses not to want to know the truth. Or that a doctor refuses to alter their medical practice to incorporate screening for hereditary cancer testing. Or they have no knowledge of the availability of the tests. Or a diagnosed cancer patient or their oncologist don't find it important after diagnosis to use test results to drive potential treatment protocols or inform other family members so they too can be tested. There a lot of reasons for someone to be missed – but the bottom line is that they all involve ignorance to some degree.

Fighting ignorance is not complicated. It involves imparting knowledge. Every day. Consistently. To anyone that will listen. It involves informing the public of their options. It involves ensuring that doctors play their role in the process of caring for and protecting the patient using all of the available weapons in their arsenal.

Obviously, hereditary cancer patients represent a relatively small portion of the overall cancer patient population. But small is still counted in thousands not tens. If tests like those produced by Myriad can identify mutations and risks and incite action *before* a cancer diagnosis, or improve the remission rate post-diagnosis by having better targeted protocols, why as a society to we continue to tolerate patients unnecessarily being sentenced to death?

Previvors, members of the population that have a hereditary cancer genetic mutation but have not gotten cancer yet, do not need to die. In fact, they don't even ever need to get cancer. Neither do any of their family members that may also possess the same mutation. And some cancer patients don't need to die either if they could receive more targeted treatments.

The tools are available to put an end to this vicious cycle. They have been provided to us by progressive, innovative companies like Myriad, who measure the success of their sales organization in terms of lives saved and not just revenues. I can't for the life of me understand why everyone isn't spreading the word. When did it become OK to not save lives? How as a society can we live with ourselves knowing that our lack of interest in educating a general population is literally causing thousands of people like Heather to leave families behind and die unnecessarily?

The buck needs to stop here. Now. If you are reading this book, the next time you hear someone talk about a history of cancer in their family, ask them if they have talked to their doctor about their potential for hereditary cancer. Ask if they have met with a genetic counselor. Ask if they have gotten a genetic screening test. And when they hesitate about the next course of action, don't let them put it off. Follow up. You never know – you may well be saving their life.

GARDEN OF EDEN

CHAPTER 18

As I grappled with a life without Heather and what it would ultimately look like, it started to become apparent that I still wasn't in a state to handle multiple complex situations and emotions. I soon realized that my calmest, most lucid moments were those times I spent in our garden, watering plants, weeding, or just simply enjoying a new flower.

Being in our garden brought me closer to Heather. It was her thing in effect. I think in a lot of ways feeling her presence almost allowed me to think clearly and 'converse' with her. It quickly became not just a way for me to honor her memory, but also a way for me to connect with her and work through the complex issues in my head. Perhaps most importantly, it allowed me to recognize that at least in the early stages of putting my life back together, simplification would be key to progress.

Before I worked at the Fortune 500 semiconductor distribution company I had been a serial entrepreneur, starting three companies over a 10 year period. I wouldn't substitute my start-up experience for anything in the world. As it turned out, the ability to compartmentalize and only focus on the fires that required immediate attention that I learned managing start-ups proved to be a most useful skill in my recovery.

Cancer has a way of stripping away all of the noise in life. It forces you to focus on the singular few things that matter. Your family. The fight. Survival.

However, if tragically the fight is lost, the focus gets lost too. In fact, for me, right after Heather died of cancer so many things were coming my way I could see how it would be completely overwhelming. The only other time that I think you remotely feel that way is when you first receive the cancer diagnosis and your whole world is thrown into disarray.

I really believe that my experience founding and managing start-ups saved me from spiraling out of control after Heather died. In the immediate period after her death, it was the gift I had to completely compartmentalize and only focus on the key things that mattered that allowed me to keep my sanity and hold the household together. I would work fast. I would accomplish things efficiently. Most importantly, I simplified. I only focused on the things that absolutely mattered at the time and compartmentalized everything else to be dealt with at a later time.

Make sure the kids would eventually be OK. Check.

Organize the Celebration of Life. Check.

Ensure paperwork and cremation was handled. Check.

Prepare and deliver the speech for Myriad. Check.

Organize an impromptu vacation with the kids to get them out of dodge for several weeks. And start the Little Mommy tradition. Check.

Every time grief would start to creep in and begin to feel like it could overwhelm me, I would take a drive. Twenty to thirty minutes in the car alone to cry would give me the time I needed to re-compartmentalize and move on to the next hottest burning fire.

I'm sure a lot of therapists (none of whom I have ever seen) would have a field day with my strategies, but compartmentalization carried me through the first 4-6 months. Every time I would get the feeling that dealing with Heather's loss was about to become the brightest burning fire, I would light a different one and re-compartmentalize. More often than not, the fires would be lit around the kids. I did everything I could to ensure that they were constantly busy and having fun. And I truly believe it worked.

Of course, eventually, I became more comfortable with the thought of letting certain fires vie for my attention. But to this day, I still use the strategy to ensure that the most important things always get done first.

There is a popular misconception that you need to be complete to be happy. For a long time for me, being busy doing good things was a perfect surrogate for happiness, which as it were, would have to wait for later.

BUSY BEES

CHAPTER 19

The first full summer after Heather died, I only knew two things:

1. I wanted to be in Rome, not in Austin on the anniversary of her death; and
2. I wanted the kids to have the trip of a lifetime around Europe spreading Little Mommies everywhere because that is what would have made Heather smile.

That is exactly what we did. On July 4th, I was in front of the Pantheon in Rome with my good friends and family and thought of Heather as I stood mesmerized at the beauty of our favorite building. Pantheon means temple to all gods – and that is what I think of when I think of Heather – she was always inclusive, never exclusive.

Over the subsequent five weeks, we went to Siena to see the Palio, an incredible horse race that has been run for hundreds of years, we revisited Florence, traveled to Athens, Sicily, Istanbul, Budapest, Prague, Venice and more. We left Little Mommies in special places everywhere. By the end of the summer, our stairwell at home was full of Nico's pictures of all of the Little Mommy locations.

We all blogged about our travels while we were in Europe. While the stories changed from person to person, the underlying theme remained the same. We were making new memories enjoying the same things we had always enjoyed when Heather was alive. She was in those memories in the form of Little Mommies. But those memories also stood on their own. For me especially, going to Europe was about starting to recognize that a future could exist that included both Heather as well as new memories that made me happy.

In essence, what I realized in Europe is that I would always love Heather and miss her. But I also discovered that I could find and have happy moments without her. And so could the kids. We could continue to create the kind of experiences in life that would honor her memory and promote our desire to never really have a bucket list and always be fulfilled.

The blogging in Europe also made me realize that my gift, my ability to write, was not only coming back, but it was coming back strong. I found myself having more and more of a desire to write. In fact, it was no longer a nice to have. Writing for me was rapidly becoming a need, an outlet, even a therapy.

I produced the most meaningful blog of the trip after our visit to Venice.

****

Last night in Venice I witnessed the most amazing fireworks display of my life. Imagine the absolute best firework display you've ever seen, then make it ten times better, put hundreds of boats in the Grand Canal, and have the beautiful Venetian skyline as the backdrop. If you do so, you will come close to giving the Redentore Festival firework display a fraction of the justice it deserves.

The multi-colored display was both artistic and awe-inspiring, and lasted an incredible 37 minutes. I thought of Heather the entire time. Since the last firework display I saw was the day Heather died, it was wonderfully therapeutic to see a firework display that for 37 minutes filled me with all of the happy memories we had, one by one erasing the awful despair that the last firework display created in me. I'm not sure I ever need to see another firework display – none of them stand even the remotest chance of measuring up. But if I ever should, I know that now fireworks will fill me with happiness, not sadness.

Honestly, it was quite unexpected that Venice would prove to be the healing portion of the trip. If Rome was sheltering and familiar, Venice was liberating and warming – a fulfilling reminder of all the great memories

Heather and I made together. Almost immediately upon our arrival, we visited the Peggy Guggenheim museum. It was great that the first painting the kids would see would be one of Heather's favorite works of Pablo Picasso, a large copy of which hangs in our bedroom. Still to this day, the Guggenheim Collection in Venice remains one of my favorite museums – a wonderful art collection in a spectacular setting. And it was fantastic to see how much the kids now appreciate it as well. Needless to say, it brought a smile to my face when Luca pointed out one of the Jackson Pollock works as one he loved – maybe he has one of my genes after all, since Pollock has always been my love, not Heather's :-)

The memories continued as we had a great lunch with my cousin Gianni at Trattoria alla Rivetta - the gondoliers' restaurant of choice. We spoke at length about Heather. Even though Gianni had only spent a small amount of time with Heather over the years, as she did with so many others, she had left a lasting impression. Gianni's description of her was perfect – an "indomitable lion" – he had perfectly understood her - her courage, pride, charisma, and desire to never give up. For some reason, speaking to Gianni of his memories of Heather proved to really set the stage for the rest of the short two-day stay in Venice.

It was truly a travel down happy memory lane. Sharing childhood memories with the kids of going to the beach near Venice with my grandparents every summer. Describing my grandmother's spirited negotiations with the fish market vendors. Showing Luca the house where his Nonno grew up. Placing a Little Mommy to rest at San Zaccaria, source for Nico's honorary Jewish name and site of my grandparents' wedding. Eating pasta with cuttlefish ink (and hearing that Nico now liked it!) and reminiscing of wonderful trips past with friends. Listening to the live music in St. Mark's square.

And many great new memories were created. Crossing the Bridge of Sighs and watching Luca's eyes get wide with fear when he heard that meant we were going to the dungeons of the Doge's Palace. Hearing Luca exclaim with excitement when he first saw "Mark Saint's Square" from our hired speedboat transferring us from the airport, connecting the dots with all the pictures his Nonno had showed him in Austin. Feeding the pigeons with leftover bread from our meals. And eating gelato after gelato until we couldn't eat any more!

As we sit in our hired car on the way to Budapest and I write this blog entry, I extend my thanks and gratitude to Venice. Thank you for being the most magnificent, unique city in the world. Thank you for housing the spirit, memories and origins of the Gabbi family. Thank you for hiding wonders down every alley and artistry on every island. Thank you for providing me with incredible seafood to eat every day. And most importantly, thank *you for giving me the Redentore and all that it means as I continue this voyage with the children.*

In short, thank you for being you. Arrivederci. Alla prossima.

****

After leaving Venice to begin the final leg of our Europe trip, in a most unexpected way in Budapest, Hungary, I realized that I had enough room in my heart to form new bonds with new women. I knew that there was no way I was ready to try and think of a woman like I had of Heather, but I did discover in Europe that I was able to talk to a woman like I did to Heather, and develop a strong bond of friendship as a result.

It sounds trivial – but recognizing that I had the ability to forge new relationships and trusted bonds was a big deal for me. The question was – how much could I translate that to my home turf? As a result of Budapest, I was able to let other new people deeper into my life after I returned from Europe that would prove to be instrumental in helping me continue to heal. The question was would it be enough?

MY GOOD IS GOOD ENOUGH

CHAPTER 20

It was a Monday a little over a year after Heather passed away. My new professional life was starting to take shape. I was right in the middle of a lecture to one of my college Marketing classes. Sixty students were listening to me intently, or at least I'd like to think they were. My phone vibrated indicating the arrival of a text message. As I always do, I sneaked a quick peak at the screen to ensure it wasn't an emergency. That is when I completely lost my composure.

On the screen was a message from my 8th grade son – it read: "Am I allowed to date?" My son had reached an important stage in his life. I quickly replied with "Define dating." His answer was the right one – "I'm not sure what you mean." So I let him know we would talk when I got home and did my best to regain my composure and talk marketing.

That night we had a long conversation. For weeks some of Nico's friends had been urging him to ask a girl out. In some ways, I think they wanted to see if he would do first what they were still afraid to do. In other ways, I think they viewed him as their leader. In yet others, I think they just had his best interest at heart – they were all convinced that the girl would say yes.

As we talked it became clear that Nico really cared about her. I knew he considered her a good friend, but it was obvious that he didn't want asking her out to mess that up. At the same time, he really wanted to ask her out. While I wanted him to do what he thought was best, I also had an additional agenda. I was happy as well – if I had to pick a first girl for him to like, it would have been her. She had been a good friend to him and a good big sister to Maya. Her younger sisters were also friends with Maya. Her father had helped me with my some of my college classes. I had helped her mother with a new business. In short, our families were pretty tightly intertwined and we got along well.

My history with women up until I met Heather had been what I would call awkward at best. For me, that hesitation almost completely stemmed from being rejected by the first girl I had ever asked out and then having my heart trampled on by my one serious high school girlfriend.

I was determined to do everything in my power to ensure that Nico's first experience would be positive. I was thrilled that he happened to like the girl he did. Other than being a good friend and a very sweet girl, based on Nico's friends' inputs, and just as importantly, a few of their mothers' intuitions, I was convinced that she would say yes. I encouraged Nico to ask her out – it would be a slam dunk I thought.

After mulling it over for a few days, he finally got the courage to do it. Much to my surprise and satisfaction, he decided he wanted to ask her in person. So I drove him to within about a block of her house and dropped him off so he could walk the rest of the way. I drove the short drive home. I was happy. He was nervous. But life was good. It was all downhill from there for both of us.

I was home for less than 30 seconds when I got the "I can't do this – come pick me up" text message. So I did. When he had turned the corner into her cul-de-sac there had been tons of other girls at her house. Understandably, he had gotten cold feet. It was one thing to have the courage to ask a girl out face to face and not hide behind text messaging, but quite another to do it in front of a ton of other girls. I honestly didn't blame him. In fact, he had already proven to be braver than I had ever been.

That night I had a work function at the house. But right before the meeting I was rewarded with his happiness –

she had given him a yes via text and he was visibly thrilled. I was both happy and relieved – for me, history had been altered. His first experience had been a positive one.

By the time my meeting adjourned, it was clear to me that something was wrong. The joy of success had been followed by the devastation of rejection.

"Dad", Nico said, "I've just been friendzoned."

"What do you mean?" I said.

Irritated, he pulled up Urban Dictionary web page to show me the definition of "friendzoned" and then showed me the girl's text message to him. She had changed her mind and her 'yes' had become a 'no'. Apparently she too really valued their friendship, but that is where it stopped for her after she thought about it some.   While I knew that in the big scheme of things, it would probably be all right, that did nothing to change Nico's palpable disappointment or assuage my fears of many awkward days ahead.

On the other hand, her 'no' to me proved to be devastating, opening the flood gates to a long series of emotions that in retrospect had probably been building for a long time, just waiting for a catalyst to ignite them.

****

When Heather was dying, my instincts told me that I would not be able to handle the overhead of being a good father, an emotionally healthy human being, and grieving for Heather. So I subscribed to the "stay busy" strategy. I overloaded myself with activities for the kids, travel planning, and work figuring that if I didn't have time to think I wouldn't have time to be depressed. I have to say that the strategy worked spectacularly well the entire time I implemented it.

About 14 months after Heather died, we had just come back from our fantastic 4 ½ week trip through Europe. I was starting a new life – new job, new company – and the kids were starting a new grade. I felt it was time to try and start moving forward – believing it would be ok to think. So I let my days return to a more normal schedule.

I didn't really notice the loneliness at first – it was very insidiously and slowly creeping into my life, taking advantage of my newfound time to think to slowly take root in my consciousness. It was waiting for a moment, a spark, to rear its head and explode.

With Nico's rejection, my loneliness was provided with the spark it had been waiting for.

* *

The chain reaction that ensued ended up being by far the worst for me since Heather's death.

I had been given the opportunity to advise Nico on one of the most important "firsts" in his life. He had talked to me and trusted me with the responsibility. For the first time, I had the opportunity to help ensure that a key part of Nico's future – his courage, his confidence – would turn out better for him than it had for me.

And I had failed him. Not only had I failed him, I had done it in monumental fashion. I had been the one that had nudged him over the edge, supremely confident that he would get a yes and that it would be good for him. And instead, I felt like I had totally let him down. Would he ever trust my advice again? How would his confidence change because of me? Would he talk to me again? These were the questions that immediately started swirling in my mind.

My failure with Nico immediately transferred into a spiraling sense of loneliness. I knew without a doubt that Heather wouldn't have screwed it up. I also knew that Heather would have been the one giving the advice. She was the one Nico talked to late into the night about his feelings. Not me. Heather was to Nico as Heather was to me. The more I thought about how right she would have gotten the same situation, and the more I blamed myself for messing it up, the more I missed her.

For the first time since I had allowed myself to think, I was overwhelmed with a feeling of loneliness and failure. If I hadn't even been able to get the first date advice right, how would I get anything else right? And with no one to lean on and talk to, where would I go to get my strength?

I had been scheduled to go to a good friend's wedding that weekend but I called it off. I just couldn't do it. I was afraid that seeing someone get married would even further push me off the deep end into realizing just how alone I was. I didn't know where to go, so I did what I normally do when I get depressed. I started crawling into my shell.

****

I have never been good at making friends. I'm an introvert at heart, so I don't find it easy to build rapport with new people. Heather had always done that for me. She screened new prospective friends and gave me a head start in getting to know them.

Also, I don't do the "sharing" and showing weakness thing very well either. There are only two people that know almost everything there is to know about me. One of them is dead and the other lives in Seattle.

Frankly, I also struggle in general with most male friendships. For some reason, I've always enjoyed a conversation with a woman more than one with a man. Maybe it's because women tend to be better listeners. Maybe it's because they are more emotionally deep. Or maybe it's because it isn't always a competition with them. Whatever it is, it was no coincidence that my best friend was a woman, and that I had married her.

****

I was stuck in a rut and didn't know what to do or where to go. As it turned out, it would be two wonderful women that helped pull me out.

Early in the morning the day following the rejection, I was terrified at how horribly awkward Nico's day would be. I texted his best friend's mother to just grease the skids on a sleepover that evening, figuring if Nico wanted to talk to someone about his experience, at this point it wouldn't be me it would probably be his best friend. Within minutes my phone rang. We talked for about an hour about the whole situation. She was stunned – she had been one of the people that was sure that the girl Nico had asked out actually liked him. It was the first time that I had told the Nico side of the story. My personal depression was building quickly. Yet it had helped to just talk and have someone say it would be ok.

Later in the day, the mother of the girl Nico had asked out dropped by my house. I'm honestly too dense to understand just how 'premeditated' her visit was, but I have to assume that some thought was put into it because it proved to be exactly the first step I needed. She came alone under the pretext of bringing me back some clothes that had been borrowed. She brought a sweet gift, what I immediately perceived (whether intended or not) as the "I know what happened and I'm not going to let anything be awkward between us" olive branch and we just chatted since Maya was around.

As we walked out to her car, in our first moment of privacy, she looked me and asked if I was ok or whether I needed to talk. It honestly caught me off guard – I kind of fumbled around and ultimately said "Not now. Maybe later." I found myself wondering how I could talk to her. What would I say – "unbeknownst to you, your daughter precipitated a sequence of events that has sent me off the emotional deep end and made me wonder if I can even keep doing this?" As circumstances would have, that is almost exactly what I told her several hours later.

****

I took a drive to the store after she left. I needed to think. And to think, I needed to get away. After reflecting, I arrived at the conclusion that my current situation was not something my best friend in Seattle could get me through. I needed a woman to talk to. For better or worse, she was the person I felt most comfortable with and thought would have the best chance of getting the whole big picture. But I still struggled with taking her up on her offer to talk – after all it was her daughter that had precipitated things. Furthermore, I was brought up in a culture and family where your problems were your problems. Families just didn't air their dirty laundry. No matter the circumstances.

It was an overwhelming feeling that I wouldn't be able to pull myself out of this one alone that pushed me over the edge. So I texted her from the parking lot of the store and asked if we could talk.

Later that night, we did. For a long time. I didn't realize how much things had been building. She proved to be a really good friend – one I really believed I could trust. And that did not come easy to me.

One of her final messages to me really resonated – she had said to never forget that "your good is good enough". It provided me with the foundation of confidence I needed that I could do this Dad thing. My kids would be just fine. Even though sometimes I would give them advice that wasn't good, overall my good would be good enough to give them what they needed. She provided me with some insight into the particular situation with Nico that helped me feel a little better. And overall, I realized that I had found a friend that I could trust that didn't live in Seattle.

She and Heather would have been good friends. They had different interests, but similar personalities. They both understood how to hear me and say what I needed to hear.

Things were definitely on the uptick by the end of the weekend. Our families had gotten together and any awkwardness there might have been between Nico and the girl or anyone else for that matter seemed to be all but gone. In the interim, Nico had talked to me and without realizing it had said exactly the right thing – he had said "Dad, you realize you gave me good advice. Things didn't work out with her and me but we're still friends. And anyone else would have given me the same advice. Everyone expected her to say yes. How could you have known any different?" My good had been good enough.

A depressing event had yielded progress. I now was beginning to believe that I could do it – I could be an effective parent without needing to be perfect. I could raise my kids in a way that would make Heather proud. I didn't have to be so hard on myself. While it would take time, I could find new people to trust. I could get to a place where I had a support network that would help me through the difficult times.

That was great progress. Only one thing remained. My support network had lives. They had families. They had spouses. They had things to do. So while I felt better, I still couldn't shake the loneliness that kept creeping in by not being busy all the time.

SOCRATES

CHAPTER 21

For years during the worst of the treatment and the time after Heather's death, I had been trying to be perfect. The perfect father (and later mother) to my children. The perfectly composed adult. The perfectly rational human being. It had been an incredible breakthrough for me to recognize that that my good would be good enough for our children. I didn't have to be the perfect Dad or a replacement Mom – if I did everything I could do, it would be good enough.

I can't overstate how liberating it had been for me to arrive at this conclusion. This freedom had been granted to me by one of the only people I had ever met that thought like Heather, understood how I thought like she did, and as a result was able to give me the right advice at the right time.

While making me feel so much better, this realization also had the perverse effect of making me recognize just how alone I really was. In other words, with progress also came regression. Two steps forward, one step back so to speak.

In her final days, this had been one of Heather's primary concerns, once again proving her incredible altruism, insight and heart. As she lay in bed slowly being consumed by cancer, her thoughts kept wandering to what I would do after she was gone. She was genuinely worried. I know she discussed her concern with many of her room visitors, not just me. I still don't know what she told them, as she was very secretive since she knew how private I was and how uncomfortable it would make me to know she was revealing our secrets to others in an effort to help.

But I do know that many of her friends were given roles – protect him, be around, help him get through it, help him find a replacement for me. They were all things that I did not want to hear about or talk about with the love of my life still alive and fighting.

As it turned out, Heather's concerns were absolutely founded. Even assuming I could get past ever imagining life with another woman other than her. Even if I stopped comparing every single woman I met to her and immediately finding flaws. Even acknowledging that I would bring somebody new into my life, be willing to share my deepest secrets, have the optimism to persevere, and the courage to risk my kids' happiness. Even if I could somehow manage to get past all of the 'if' statements, and they were big ones, Heather knew it would be a struggle for me. In other words, Heather knew enough about me to know that even a healthy me would struggle to bring any new real friends into my life, let alone a new woman.

As always, she had been totally right about me. My inability to admit this to her as she was dying didn't change the reality that both she and I knew existed. Heather knew how socially awkward I was. With extremely few exceptions, I had always relied on her to make my friends. As incapable as I was of forging new relationships and making small talk, Heather could be best friends with a room full of people in the time it took me to get the courage to even walk in through the door.

Beyond my awkwardness, I lacked the self-confidence and trust to create new bonds. I had just been burned, betrayed or rejected too many times by supposed friends.

Ironically, my supreme confidence in professional and academic settings contrasted starkly with my utter lack of confidence in social settings. I had no problem lecturing to a room of 500 people, leading a sales team, or bouncing back from a rejection to go close the next big sales deal. But I squirmed at the thought of having to find something to talk about with someone I didn't know or being the odd person out at a party.

Perhaps that had been an underlying reason I had been so upset about Nico's initial rejection and that it had precipitated so much for me – it may have hit too close to home. It may have been a reminder of my personal failures and how much I didn't want any of my kids experiencing those things, especially the one that had the most similar personality. I guess it's the destiny of a parent – we can't help seeing ourselves in our children.

As I was contemplating what on Earth my alternatives were and flirting with another trip down depression lane, I came across a card that was sent to me by my colleagues in Hungary right after Heather's passing. In the card they had hand-written a quote by the famous Greek philosopher Socrates. It read:

"The secret of change is to focus all of your energy not on fighting the old but on building the new."

Seeing that quote convinced me that it was time for me to take the next step and build the new. Now that I had come to grips with the fact that my good would be good enough for parenting, and I had started anew with my career, transitioning from a Fortune 200 management position back to start-ups and full-time teaching at the University, all that I had left to do was figure out what the "new" me would look like.

As unfair as it was to her, I felt there was only one place I could go – to the woman who had already gotten me to the point I was. I just hoped that I wouldn't wear out my welcome. I needed her to get through whatever it was I was supposed to get through. I felt like she could help me get there a lot more quickly than anyone else.

FACEBOOK THINKS I'M GAY

CHAPTER 23

It had been a breakthrough for me to determine that I needed to get somewhere new for myself. The problem was I didn't really know where "there" was. Who would be my friends? I was a single Dad with a situation that no one liked to talk about. For couples, I would be a third wheel that frequently enjoyed hanging with the women more than the men – a recipe for awkward. I tried meeting women that shared a similar story to mine. That was always great for one coffee because we were guaranteed to relate but then tended to turn awkward or depressing real fast. I even tried catering to my strengths – meeting professionals. That turned awkward the second things got personal. I honestly was clueless. I had no idea what to do.

So I started stagnating again. It took a couple of things happening to make me realize that whatever new was going to be, I needed to get on it, and quick.

One day I was going through my Facebook newsfeed and I suddenly realized that the vast majority of the ads being presented to me were for gay bars in Austin. The implication hit me after only a brief delay – "Oh for Pete's sake" I thought, "Facebook thinks I'm gay." I began laughing hysterically.

Anyone that knows me knows that I'm a natural storyteller. I love recounting experiences in a humorous way and putting on a show. This almost immediately became my new showpiece. I would tell anyone that would listen – "Facebook thinks I'm gay."

But then all of a sudden humor started transforming into a more somber tone. It began occurring to me that if Facebook thought I was gay then I really didn't have much of a social life other than hanging out with my gay friends. In fact, the more I thought about it, the more I realized that my only activity in the months since I had returned from Europe (and frankly since well before we had left for Europe) had been to periodically go out to dinner with my gay friends, or play strategy games with a group of 8th graders that my son Nico is friends with.

Don't get me wrong – I truly enjoyed and still have a great time with both activities. I wouldn't substitute good food and friends or the opportunity to hang out in a meaningful way with my son and his friends for anything. It wasn't that I was looking to stop doing those things, it just became clear that I couldn't continue to survive strictly in the status quo.

But there's a big difference between problem recognition and resolution. I honestly didn't know what to do. I knew it was time to get out. But I didn't know how. I wanted meaningful relationships – I'm not capable of small talk. I wanted to be able to love again, both romantically and platonically, but I still wanted to be sure I stayed in love with the past. I wasn't sure how I would allow for all of these things to coexist. To be perfectly honest, I began to feel guilty for even having those thoughts. Not living my life 100% for Heather somehow felt like a betrayal to her, even though the emotion was unfounded and I knew she would feel that way as well. This would prove to be one of the most difficult problems to date I would need to solve.

****

It's difficult to describe how easy it is to spiral downward when you're alone. In my opinion, daily life in general is an emotional cycle. There are always ups and downs. The problem I believe with being alone is that it has a way of affecting the amplitude of the emotional cycle. When good things happen to you, they feel a little less good because you have no one to share the happy moment or success with. When you have a relatively tougher day, it has a way of becoming worse because no one is there to help soften the blow. The net result of the goods being slightly less good and the downs being a little more down is a slight but definite downward slope to the worse over time from an emotional perspective.

It took me seemingly forever to figure this out. The realization hit me one evening the day after I had just come back from a trip to visit Myriad. On several occasions since the speech in Las Vegas, I had the opportunity to travel to Salt Lake City to visit Myriad headquarters. Every time I would make the trip they would help me find the time to address a group of people and tell Heather's story. This time, I had recounted our family's story to a group of employees from headquarters and a set of new salespeople that had just completed their onboarding training. As had been the case with every other time I had done it, the immediate emotional response from delivering the talk was one of jubilation at knowing that Heather's story would drive more people to save more lives. However, reliving Heather's story and watching people moved to tears by it always had consequences for me later.

Jubilation at some point slowly morphed into the sadness of having to relive all of the things that had happened to me over and over again. It never really got any easier, but I knew I could never stop doing the right thing even if it would potentially allow me to move on less painfully. The fact that I had no one to share the jubilation with made it a little less powerful. Similarly, the fact that I had no one to soften the sadness made it a little worse.

After my return home to Austin, my sadness deepened. Only this particular time, I wasn't able to find a distraction to alleviate it. My kids didn't want to go out and do something with me to take my mind off of it. I didn't tell them how I was feeling. I thought it would be unfair to burden them with the truth and didn't want them to go out for the wrong reasons as that would have probably made me feel worse.

Not surprisingly, as was frequently the case, the phone didn't ring either. With no outlet for my sadness, it only grew worse over the course of the day. Finally, by the time the sun set I finally just got in my car and left my house. I thought it might do me some good to think about what was happening, and typically for me driving time served that purpose well. It was during this drive that I finally figured the emotional cycle out.

I was sure that at least understanding the pattern would help me better deal with it in the future. I resolved to try and ensure that in the future I did a better job sharing my happy moments with others to further enrich them and make the good part of the cycle better. I also promised myself to at least try and prepare for the predictable moments of sadness by readying a distraction that would help make the downs a little less severe.

Unfortunately, while those would prove to be reasonable stop-gap measures, I still didn't have a long-term solution. To me, having a long-term solution meant having the phone ring with people that actually wanted to be with me and hear about my successes, be my friend, and help me through my sadness. For the cycle to break, I needed to stop being the one asking for help, and instead needed to possess a sustainable ecosystem of friends where communication was bidirectional. Longer term, it meant finding someone that I knew would always be there for me, friend, girlfriend or wife, without my having to ask.

As always, recognition of the problem and resolution were a universe apart. I couldn't make people want to call me. Moreover, I certainly couldn't conjure someone up that would always want to be there for me. So I sat in a restaurant alone (always a source of depression for me even when Heather was alive), watching a football game, writing this chapter of the book, wondering what I could do. I didn't come up with any answers. I didn't even come up with a single good idea. I was still at square one.

FALLING TO PIECES

CHAPTER 24

There is a song I really like by a band called The Script. Even though the overall song doesn't really apply to my situation, every time I listen to it on the radio there is a line in the song that always sticks with me:

"What am I supposed to do when the best part of me was always you?"

That is truly how I have felt since Heather and I even started dating. She was always the person in the relationship that brought everything from the outside to the table: new friends, experiences, adventures, and fun. I think that in no small part my inability to solve my 'Facebook' problem directly related to the fact that I had always relied on Heather to build relationships for me. She was very much the central hub of the Gabbi family and the ultimate social coordinator. At some point, my reliance on her for all my relationships had translated into a conviction on my part that I wasn't any good at them, or frankly even capable of starting them. After her death, I found myself frequently questioning who would even want to hang out with me. In fact, I really started to wonder who would even want to put up with me, a still damaged man trying to find his way back into a 'normal' life.

****

I kept waiting and waiting to write this chapter. The rest of my manuscript had been pretty much done for some time, and this chapter still just contained just a title and a very basic note to myself that read: "Open ended answer – still not resolved."

It ultimately took a phone conversation with one of Heather's closest friends to help me recognize the best way to bring this chapter to life. She had been one of my first manuscript readers - I had ultimately tired of waiting and sent out the book with the unfinished chapter for review.

We talked about the stories she felt were still missing from the book and then I asked her about her overall impressions. She told me that she had finished reading the book and immediately found herself wanting the sequel because she wanted to know what happened next to me. I almost instantly realized that this had been the answer I was looking for all along for this chapter.

My journey wasn't even close to over yet. With this chapter, I was subconsciously trying to create an ending to a book that didn't deserve, require or need one yet. My life was still a work in progress, as was my healing process. The fact that I didn't yet have a collection of friends who actually wanted to be around me because of who I was rather than who I had been married to just meant that story wasn't ready for telling yet, not that it would never be told.

That story would have to be in the sequel she had referred to. Instead of it bothering me that I hadn't been able to neatly wrap everything up, realizing that my life was still a work in process and that some things just had to be figured out in their own time, was quite liberating. Because in my heart of hearts, I knew they would be.

I wanted a sequel. In fact, I knew I needed a sequel. But at that point, just recognizing that a portion of my journey could be gauged as complete while still leaving room for further progress was comforting enough for me, even if not totally fulfilling.

THE ROAD NOT TAKEN

CHAPTER 25

THE ROAD NOT TAKEN

By Robert Frost

Two roads diverged in a yellow wood,

And sorry I could not travel both

And be one traveler, long I stood

And looked down one as far as I could

To where it bent in the undergrowth;

Then took the other, as just as fair,

And having perhaps the better claim,

Because it was grassy and wanted wear;

Though as for that the passing there

Had worn them really about the same,

And both that morning equally lay

In leaves no step had trodden black.

Oh, I kept the first for another day!

Yet knowing how way leads on to way,

I doubted if I should ever come back.

I shall be telling this with a sigh

Somewhere ages and ages hence:

Two roads diverged in a wood, and I—

I took the one less traveled by,

And that has made all the difference.

This poem by Robert Frost had always been Heather's favorite. It is the poem I chose to have engraved on the urn on my mantle that holds the portion of Heather's ashes that did not take on the form of Little Mommies. Along with the poem, a hummingbird is also engraved on the urn. I think those two things just as much as anything else epitomize Heather. The energy and flittering about of a hummingbird and the meaning of the poem describe her philosophy on life perfectly. I am proud to say that because I had the privilege of being who Heather chose to love for almost 20 years, they also now describe my philosophy on life.

To us both, life is about experiences. It is about seeking out what is different, learning about it, assimilating it, and appreciating it for what it is. Diversity teaches tolerance. Diversity allows for innovation and new thinking. Diversity is the key to everything.

Before I met Heather, I was all about taking the road most travelled. When presented with a choice of laying on the couch or getting out and experiencing something new, I chose the couch. When presented with novelty, I instead opted for habit. Rather than actively seek things that made me uncomfortable, I chose to remain in my comfort zone.

Heather opened my eyes to the benefits of taking risks. She supported my frequently crazy business ideas. She was the one who always encouraged people to pursue knowledge for its own sake. To always be inquisitive. To not necessarily choose the best path, the most logical path, or the most accepted path. Heather always sought and encouraged individuality in people. She forced them to expand their minds, whether it was talking to 3rd graders about Joan Miro' and Pablo Picasso during their Spanish lessons, or developing a love for hiking in me, or even taking the kids to a local ice cream factory. In fact, one of her best friends reminded me that Heather's quest for knowledge sometimes bordered on the comically absurd – as in when she dissected one of our goldfish that had died to try and determine the cause of death!

Heather not only always took the road less traveled herself, but she consistently encouraged others to do so. Frequently, she brought people along on the voyage with her. I cannot even think of how many lives she touched in this way.

But I can say that I have tried to live up to the high bar she set by being a guide to others down the road less traveled. Whether I'm in a classroom trying to teach a group of college undergraduates how to think about marketing in a different way or trying to get people to make their first trip to Europe with me to get them hooked on traveling, I constantly try and lead people down this path.

I have even tried to formalize the process. I can emulate Heather but I will never be her. I don't possess the spontaneity. So instead what I've tried to do is take the basic premise we both agreed on – help people develop a desire to seek and embark upon the road less traveled – and make it my own.

This is perhaps most evident in the extracurricular activities I have structured for my kids and some of their friends, which is now in its second year. Heather and I are both believers that exposure to many different things is what makes well-rounded human beings, and that diversity is what makes the world go around.

In my first year, I taught six 7th graders how to start a business and taught eight 4th graders to appreciate all aspects of the arts – literature, art, theater, music, movies, and more. This year, I am taking ten 5th graders on a voyage around the world with my Globetrotters program and helping ten 8th graders develop, film, produce, and promote a short film to raise funds for charity.

A key part of my start-up involves paying it forward to the local community. The business allocates a percentage of its profits to provide scholarships to disadvantaged youth interested in pursuing entrepreneurial ventures, as well as classes to middle school and high school students to teach them how to become successful entrepreneurs. Effectively, the social component of my new business, Global Innovation Village, is all about helping people navigate the road less traveled.

I continue to actively pursue any behavior that helps people fulfill their desire to attempt new things, explore new talents, and embark on new adventures as I believe that this truly does the memory of Heather justice.

LESSONS FROM THE TRENCHES

CHAPTER 26

I had planned to save this chapter for last, assuming it would be the easiest to write. My thought was that it would simply be a collection of the most valuable lessons I have learned throughout the process as it has unfolded so far. I didn't realize how hard it would actually be to try and condense all of the experiences that this tragedy has given me into a few brilliant take-home lessons that people affected by this in the future could use as a guide.

In fact, it actually took me a few weeks to come to the realization that my original idea for this chapter of the book would be impossible to deliver upon. To try and condense this book into a few generalized bullet points would be doing a disservice to all those who have lived through this process. It would be ignoring the fact that each family's situation is unique. It is a collection of the personal experiences, situation, and emotion that the players in that process have. Pretending to understand what others are going through would be an insult to the uniqueness of the love in their family.

Instead, what I have chosen to do is provide a summary of the things that I have learned and that have helped me at least get to the point in the healing process that I am today. I do this not to suggest that they will work for others, but rather to hopefully provide you with ideas that you may be able to modify to suit your needs and apply to your own personal situation. If, as Ella gave me the idea of collecting written memories, one of the ideas I bring forth helps you or a loved one better deal with a situation you are facing, then I will have succeeded in my purpose for this chapter.

In no particular order, here is a my top list of the things that I have come to realize over a long process filled with tragedy, sadness, happiness, hope, and more than a few drives to think.

❖ **PICK UP THE KEYS AND DRIVE THE BUS**
    Take ownership of your treatment program and find as many people and options as you can to ride the bus with you. Nobody will care about you more than you and your family, so why would you leave the most important decisions in your life to someone else? One of the most important things Heather and I did was take this process

over very early on. Other than helping us ensure we did everything we could to survive, it helped me have no regrets or guilt after her death, wondering whether I could have done more. I knew we had done it all because we had driven the bus the entire time.

❖ MANAGE THE HELP

We have the tendency to not want to impose on people and ask for help. Get over it. Cancer is overwhelming enough as it is. No one should have to face it alone. Identify the different kinds of people that want to help and systematically use each kind to its fullest. That doesn't make you a bad person. It makes you someone who is doing everything they can to make it through the process. Ella's greatest gift to us was to allow us to learn this very early in the process. This approach ensured that we had the things we needed every step of the way so Heather and I could single-mindedly focus on the most important tasks at hand.

❖ TRUST IN THE TRUTH

Never underestimate the ability of your kids or loved ones to process and handle the truth. It might be more painful in the long run, but would you rather they understand the process and work through it or one day be shocked by the outcome and not have the time to do, say, and ask all the things they wanted to? Don't steal memories from your kids or family members to shield them emotionally. I strongly believe both you and they will end up regretting it later. Even though they have had to live through an unfair amount of tragedy at their young age, I believe my three kids are so well adjusted because they were able to truly live through the process with their mother. They were able to fit in a lot of conversations that they wouldn't have been able to have had we not been honest from the beginning. I know this is something they will be increasingly grateful for as they continue to grow up.

❖ **SIMPLIFY AND COMPARTMENTALIZE**
Superheroes don't exist. Which means you aren't one of them either. It's okay to admit that handling everything at one time would completely overwhelm you. When things feel like they might be getting out of control, simplify. Zero in on only those fires that require your immediate attention and compartmentalize the rest for further review. This doesn't mean that you're ignoring their existence. It means you are saying that you will not address them until you can give them the attention they deserve. For me, staying busy for the first six months and compartmentalizing my emotions allowed me to

ensure that the kids were taken care of, that I truly understood the legacy I wanted to leave, and that the right foundation had been put in place upon which I could rebuild my life.

❖ **DO WHAT WORKS FOR YOU**
Everyone is different. Every family has different experiences, emotions, and history. Each individual is unique. That's what makes us human. So be cautious about taking any prescription from anyone, including mine, and directly making it your own. Ask yourself what elements of the advice apply to your particular situation, think about it, and modify it to best suit your unique situation. I took the idea of capturing memories and photos from friends for a memory book verbatim from Ella's family, but I came up with the idea of canisters of ashes to satisfy a unique need that my family and I had.

❖ **BUILD MEMORIES OLD AND NEW**
Balance your time between doing things that help keep the memory of your loved one alive and making new memories with them. I believe this is particularly important for children. As they grow up, it is much easier to tell them stories about their loved one if they have been making new memories with them <u>after</u> their death. My four year old son Luca won't really have many of his

own memories of Heather from the time before she died. But placing Little Mommies around the world is allowing him to form a bond with her that is his own, and not imparted on him by me, that he will be able to cherish for the rest of his life.

❖ **FOLLOW THE ROAD LESS TRAVELED**
At any time in life, don't be afraid to take chances, move outside of your comfort zone, and try new things. This was Heather's greatest gift to me, and it is especially true as you are trying to heal from the tragedy that has befallen you and move forward. You will be forced into situations that you aren't comfortable with or have never thought about. I know it's very easy to say, but don't fear them. Embark on the journey down the road less traveled with courage and excitement. The more you do the easier it will become. I am honestly still uncomfortable in new situations, but I have recognized that this is the only way that I will be able to complete the healing process and rebuild my life.

❖ **REMOVE THE 'UN' FROM YOUR LIFE**
Do your best every day to keep your bucket list empty. You never know when life might through you a curve ball. If you constantly try to remove the 'un' from your life, then no matter when it

ends you will have no regrets. As a survivor, that could make all the difference for you. I know that for Heather and me it was liberating to know that we truly had nothing left to say or do. It somehow made things a little easier to deal with when we didn't have to travel down the "what if" highway. What if we had done this different? What if we had actually taken this chance? What if we had waited to go on this trip?

❖ **KNOW WHAT YOU WANT YOUR LEGACY TO BE AND THEN DRIVE TOWARD IT**

Life is more about what you do for others than what you do for yourself. Ask yourself periodically what you want your legacy to be. Really think about the answer. Then single-mindedly drive your activities toward the fulfillment of your legacy. You will end up being much happier. Moreover, you will find yourself fulfilled and approaching life every day with the passion to live, love and laugh. When I started directing all of the activities in my life toward making a difference for others, my perspective immediately changed. I found happy moments easier to come by. I found that I was approaching every situation with more energy, passion and optimism. In short, when I started living life around fulfilling my legacy, life started feeling good again. And I began to realize that it would be possible for me to be happy again.

❖ **FIND A SPECIAL PLACE FOR YOU AND YOUR LOVED ONE**
There will be times during which you will want to 'talk' to your loved one. You will want to feel close to them. You will want their presence to help you through a difficult situation, process, or emotion. Be sure to have a special place for you to accomplish this. It should be private, have special meaning, and make you instantly feel close to them. For me, this is Heather's garden. Being out in our landscape, working in the garden, almost instantly makes me feel at peace and close to her. It has a calming influence on me and allows me to rediscover my equilibrium if things start getting out of kilter in my life. Sometimes just finding peace is all that you need to begin moving forward again.

I AM

CHAPTER 27

I am still sad every so often. But there are many more happy days for me now than there are sad ones.

I am not perfect. But I am now at peace with the knowledge that my good will almost always be good enough.

I am still haunted by the fact that were it not for one doctor, my wife might still be here with me and my kids may well still have a mother. But I have chosen to look past this and move forward rather than regret what has already happened.

Perhaps most importantly, I am hopeful. And while hope may not be a strategy, it is the feeling that every day allows me to get up and persevere. Hope allows me to see a day in the future when no unnecessary lives are lost to cancer. It allows me to envision a day in which my kids grow up and start their own families. It allows me see a life for myself that is more filled with happiness than loneliness.

I am healing.

I am making a difference.

I am going to be okay.

EPILOGUE

This book was written over a period of four months. In some ways, it was the hardest thing I've ever done. Putting my emotions and my healing process down on paper acknowledged its existence more than anything else I could have done. Frequently, this recognition caused more emotional pain than I felt like I could handle. But in retrospect, I don't think I could have truly begun healing without doing it.

As it turns out, virtual pen and paper were the friend I had been looking for. They were also there to listen to me when I had something to say. They were patient. They allowed me to express my emotions without judgment. Whether a single person ever reads this book, it will have served its purpose for me. It has allowed me to understand where I've been, make sense of it, and plan out where I need to go next to reconstruct my life and try and find true happiness again.

Of course, if this book is truly successful, I will also be fulfilling my legacy to make a difference. I will be helping other people find peace and cope with the potentially unfair situation they are being cast into. I will be inspiring others to journey down the road less traveled. I will be spreading Heather's influence and philosophy of life to others all over. I will be saving lives by imparting the knowledge of hereditary cancer screening on someone who could benefit from it who may otherwise have not considered it. I will be changing perspectives on what it means to truly live without a bucket list.

Finally, with every copy sold, I will be providing financing to Wonders & Worries so that they are in a position to help more and more children cope with the serious illness of a loved one. For this reason, if you feel like this book has proven itself worthy of attention, I would like to implore you to help spread the word. This book is self-published. Word will only get out if readers like you who are grateful for the experience and advice help publicize it and its message to your community around you.

Thank you for allowing me to take you on my emotional roller coaster. I hope your experience riding it was as meaningful as my journey describing it to you.

Sincerely,

Alex Gabbi (Austin, Texas 2014)

ABOUT THE AUTHOR

Alex Gabbi is a devoted father to his wonderful three kids, Nico, Maya, and Luca, ages 13, 11, and 4. After his wife Heather died, he gave up a successful career in  business to focus on making a difference for others in the community in as many ways as possible, including teaching at the McCombs School of Business at The University of Texas at Austin, spreading the word on hereditary cancer, and supporting Wonders & Worries, an Austin-based non-profit focused on helping children better cope when one of their parents has a serious illness.

In fact, 30% of the proceeds from The Journey will be donated to Wonders & Worries.

Alex lives in Austin, Texas and may be reached at thejourney@alexgabbi.com.

36900937R00113

Made in the USA
Lexington, KY
09 November 2014